THE BEGINNER'S GUIDE TO Painting Watercolors

Rosemary Williams

Commissioned artwork by Elaine Alderson

BISON GROUP

First published in 1993 by
Bison Books Ltd
Kimbolton House
117A Fulham Road
London SW3 6RL

ISBN 1-85841-006-1

Printed in Hong Kong
Reprinted 1994

PAGE 1
Antonia Black
Roosters
Watercolor

PAGE 2/3
Antonia Black
Camel Tenders in Tunisia
Watercolor

PAGE 4/5
Kevin Chapman
Riverside 1
Mixed media

Contents

Introduction

Watercolor: A Beginner's Guide is a practical book designed to entice students with all levels of ability to learn how to paint in the medium for their own pleasure. Many people who enjoy or wish to learn painting are not able to attend art classes. This book will take them step by step through a series of simple exercises and projects, explaining both the theories and the techniques in a practical way. These will build together to form a progressive and sequential course.

Contrary to popular belief, painting and drawing can be taught just like reading and writing, through exploring and practicing aspects fundamental to the subject. As you work on the examples suggested here, your ability and confidence will develop.

A range of watercolor media are discussed here, including pure watercolor, gouache, inks and acrylics. Techniques relevant to all these are presented at two different levels. The basic level offers examples of simple exercises relevant to any watercolor technique. These are coupled with examples of work by professional artists and teachers, together with diagnostic comments. The section on further techniques can be used as a follow-up chapter, or the more advanced artist can dip into it for ideas as required.

The book begins with a broad historical overview, showing how the exciting advances of the nineteenth and twentieth centuries have influenced ideas and techniques. This is followed by a core of basic information and theories linked to practical examples dealing with drawing, perspective, composition and the use of color. Finally a small selection of paintings is included for pure enjoyment to illustrate the broad applications of the medium and to stimulate ideas through which you can extend your working horizons.

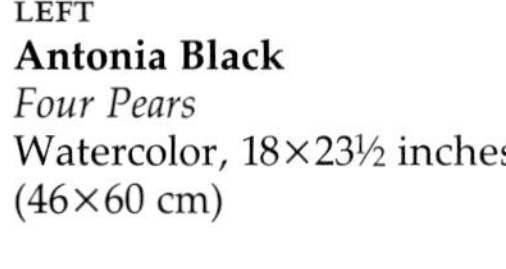

LEFT
Antonia Black
Four Pears
Watercolor, 18×23½ inches (46×60 cm)

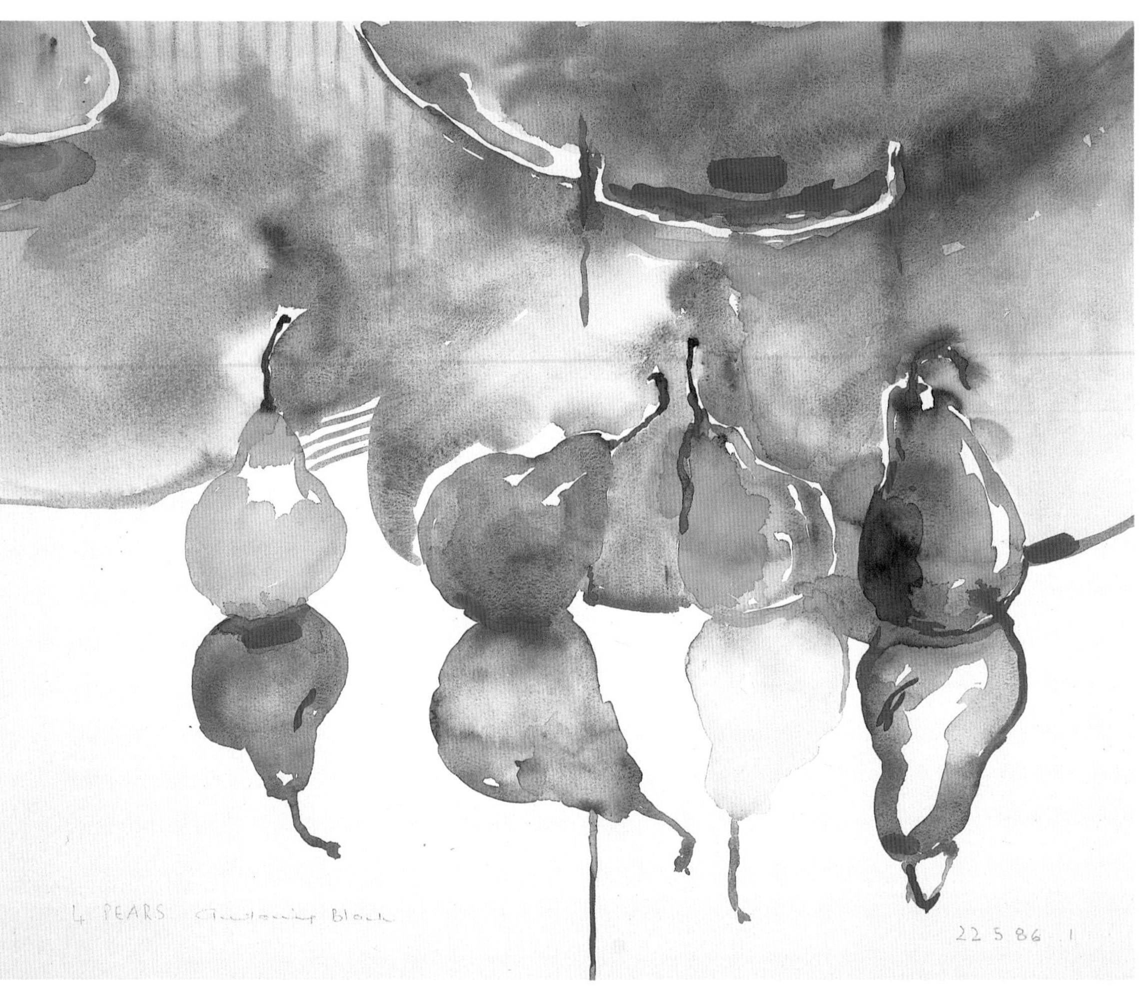

RIGHT
David Wise
View of Hastings with a Bowl of Fruit
Watercolor, 29¾×22 inches (76.2×56.3cm)
This is a celebration of rich color and love of pattern. The scale of the still life is small in comparison with the rest of the painting, yet it boldly holds its position in the composition against the distorted perspective of the table top. The ellipses of the intense blue plate change the flattened space into a more stable realistic plane so that the solid fruit can be supported by it. The rest of the painting is predominantly green and red, with a little softer blue echoed up through the view of the houses outside. The window frame fits snugly into the proportion of the paper and the touches of blue flicker around it like a neon sign. The eye is led around and into the view, yet it constantly returns to the still life inside the room. The perspective is deliberately distorted and flattened to enhance the spacious tension between the realism of the still life and the stylization of the view.

1. Historical Factors

Watercolor is a vibrant and exciting medium with a long and expressive tradition which reflects all the major movements and influences in the history of art. Its roots can be found in the art of ancient civilizations dating from the beginning of time. As we near the advent of the next millennium it is clear that artists are still captivated by the challenge of its flexible and versatile properties, and its range and possibilities are still being developed.

The earliest record of watercolor is in the cave paintings found at Altamira and Lascaux. Pigments of rich ocher and red were made from colored clay, black from burnt woods. The resulting tribal images of bison and antelope are still clear and colorful today. Many ancient civilizations used natural colors from the earth and plants mixed with gums to make a lasting and beautiful paint with which to depict their everyday life or symbolic and magical patterns exclusive to their tribes.

The Egyptians as early as 2500BC used fresco techniques of watercolor on plaster to decorate their tombs and buildings. This method was developed to a pinnacle of perfection by the masters of the Italian Renaissance in the fifteenth and sixteenth centuries. Perhaps the most famous fresco/watercolor is the ceiling of the Sistine Chapel by Michelangelo (1475-1564). Major artists who also developed the medium in its own right include Albrecht Dürer (1471-1528), whose delicate observations of plants and animals used transparent washes developed with line, and opaque color overlaid for the fine details.

Rubens (1577-1640) and Rembrandt (1606-1669) of the Dutch School used vigorous, free line and wash or local color as a method of gathering information on a subject to be used in subsequent paintings or etchings. They influenced the English School, including Hogarth (1697-1764) and Gainsborough (1727-1788), who used watercolor to record observations of people on location, and Constable (1776-1837) and Turner, who wanted to record the ever-changing effects of weather and light on the landscape. Their innovatory techniques were developed in response to the subtle moods of the English landscape.

Lesser artists who practiced brilliantly the traditional skills of watercolor as the center of their work included, among many others, Thomas Girtin (1775-1802), John Sell Cotman (1782-1842) and David Cox (1783-1859). They perfected the British Style so well suited to the landscape of England. Their works inspired a rising tide of amateur interest. Watercolor as a pure medium was not popular elsewhere until the latter half of the nineteenth century. Handmade papers and paints were generally difficult to find, whereas in England the demand led to manufacturers such as William Reeves and James Whatman producing ready-sized hand-made papers and portable cakes of paint.

Many people think that watercolor was invented in the eighteenth century, when it became controled and formalized through the popularity of Paul Sandby (1725-1809). His delicate topographical studies of major architectural sites such as Windsor Castle were painted with transparent watercolor giving the details of the drawing a magical luminosity. Sandby is known as 'the father of English watercolor'. He encouraged the newly rich and cultured gentlemen to practise the art as they toured Europe.

BELOW
John Constable RA
(1776-1837)
Stonehenge (1835)
Watercolor
Constable used watercolor in a strikingly bold and impressionistic manner to record his detailed and direct observations of the English countryside.

The Industrial Revolution of 1750-1850 led to watercolor painting and collecting becoming accessible and attractive to the amateur painter. This in turn led to the imposition of the rigorous self-restraint synonymous with Victorian values. Watercolor techniques became controled and limited; layers of translucent washes used without any white became the only recognized style. Colors were limited to three or four, with subtle mixes made through the combination of layers of pigments. The expressive, vigorous and emotional watercolor style, built on inspiration and a sensitive response to the landscape, of Turner and Constable became outmoded. This was totally opposed to the climate of the nineteenth-century English watercolor, whose correct

ABOVE
Paul Sandby (1725-1809)
Windsor Castle: North Terrace Looking West at Sunset
Watercolor
Sandby's luminous topographical studies gave watercolor a new and fashionable prominence in the mid-eighteenth century.

LEFT
Rembrandt van Rijn (1606-69)
Farmstead by a Stream
Reed pen and brown ink
Rembrandt used line and wash or ink for preliminary sketches which he later expanded into paintings or etchings.

ABOVE
Vassily Kandinsky
(1866-1944)
Untitled (1910)
Graphite and watercolor,
19½×25¼ inches
(49.6×64.8cm)
This small untitled watercolor is regarded as perhaps the first non-figurative abstract painting, and as such is a milestone in the history of art, a rare distinction for a water-based medium.

RIGHT
Paul Cézanne (1839-1906)
Montagne Sainte-Victoire
(1905-6)
Watercolor on paper,
14¼×21⅝ inches
(36.5×55.3cm)
Cézanne's watercolors were profoundly influential on twentieth-century painting.

and structured rules still seem to be the model for many beginners and amateurs today. This makes the innovations and ideas of the twentieth-century masters doubly exciting.

From 1820 major French artists such as Théodore Géricault and Eugène Delacroix discovered the work of Turner, Constable and Richard Parkes Bonnington, the latter inspiring a large following in France. By the end of the century, the medium was popular with the Impressionists, including Edouard Manet and Pierre Auguste Renoir, who both developed a sensitive technique.

Two artists who made major contributions to the emergence of a new ideology and who developed their techniques in watercolor were Paul Cézanne (1839-1906) and Auguste Rodin (1840-1917). They were brilliant exponents of the medium of watercolor, although best known for their works in other media. The sculptor Rodin used watercolor to work out his ideas, and as an extension to his drawing. His commonest subject was the female figure in fluid athletic or dancing poses, captured with the simplest of free flowing lines and washes. The resulting images seemed poised to return to life.

Cézanne worked with watercolor from the beginning of his career, but it is in the late works that his ideas were most fully realized. The white paper became fundamental to the content of the picture. It was a statement both about spatial values and about the value of the surface of the paper. The marks of both pencil and paint existed with integrity and in their own right; together they recreated the space and the subject within it. Form in Cézanne's paintings was created through primary color modulations in many decisive, selective marks which brought the white surface to life. The paintings seem both to create and dissolve form at the same time. They profoundly influenced the direction of Cubism and twentieth-century painting as a whole.

George Grosz (1893-1959) was exposed to Cubism and Futurism in 1913 and he became one of the most important watercolorists of the new century. His talent lay in this medium alone and he used all its seductive techniques to make a social commentary on war and Nazi oppression; he fled to America in 1933. He was able to conjure up the fabric of life with a few strokes of wet-into-wet pigment. The sheer sensuality of the paint mixture was juxtaposed with satirical and subversive images.

Watercolor has been used extensively throughout the twentieth century by all the major masters of Modernism, who have broken out of the narrow and formal constraints imposed by the pure watercolorists of the early nineteenth century. Pablo Picasso, Paul Klee, George Grosz, Wassily Kandinsky, Jackson Pollock, Marc Rothko, David Hockney and many others have all worked consistently with the medium, experimenting and developing new ideas and techniques. Nonetheless few pure watercolors are cited as major examples of twentieth-century painting. This distinction is given to works in oils and, later, acrylics. There is one notable exception in a small untitled watercolor made in 1910 by Kandinsky, which is regarded as possibly the first nonfigurative abstract painting and a major milestone in the development of twentieth-century art. It is ironic that the gentlemanly 'English Art' of the cultured Victorian amateur should hold such a revolutionary place in the history of art.

BELOW
George Grosz (1893-1959)
Street Fight From the Roof (1934)
Watercolor on wove paper, 25¾×19 inches (66×48.7cm)
Addison Gallery of American Art, gift of the artist (1943.30)
One of the major watercolorists of the twentieth century, Grosz used all the subtlety of the medium to launch a savage attack on Fascism.

2. Materials and Equipment

Papers

Papers are available in many qualities and grades and the choice of paper directly influences the final results. Students may work on cheap cartridge or unstretched paper, and then find that the surface is buckling, creating real problems in applying and controlling the paint. Cheaper cartridge papers are ideal for preliminary drawing and for following the drawing exercises outlined in this book; they are bound like sketchbooks.

Hand Made Papers

These are more absorbent, have a more textured surface, and are heavier in weight than cartridge. There are three standard types available, and the choice will be based on grade, weight, color and size in relation to personal preference and the type of painting to be made. The very best and most expensive papers are made from pure linen rags, while intermediate qualities will include both linen and cotton in their manufacture.

Weight

Papers are graded by their weight in pounds per ream (480 sheets) or grams per square meter (GSM). The most popular weight is 72lb (150gsm), a thinnish paper. Wrinkling can occur when thin paper is wet so it must be stretched prior to applying paint. Heavier weights such as 140lb or 200lb plus can be worked on without prior stretching unless the technique involves a lot of water.

Size

The UK and the US retain the traditional imperial sizes for high-quality hand made papers; all other papers, such as cartridge drawing paper, use the international A sizes.

Imperial
Double Elephant 27x40in (686x1001mm)
Imperial 22x30in (559x762mm)
½ Imperial 22x15in (381x559mm)
Royal 19½x25in (490x610mm)

'A' Sizes
A1 23½x33in (594x840mm)
A2 16½x23½ (420x594mm)
A3 11¾x16½in (297x420mm)
A4 8¼x11¾in (210x297mm)
A5 5⅞x8¼in (148x210mm)

Color

Paper is available in a range of colors, although white is the most commonly used for watercolors as it is transparent. Tinted paper provides an overall background tone, giving the painting a sense of unity. Gouache or poster paints, which are opaque, can be used effectively on tinted papers.

Right Side of Paper

All papers have a right/wrong side. This is usually obvious because of the watermark, but if in doubt touch a corner of the paper to your lip and the sized side will feel very slightly tacky.

Papers are the foundation to a painting; explore and experiment with them, relate the imaginary to them as artists have through-

Paper surfaces

Hot Pressed (HP) has a smooth absorbent surface and is excellent for line and wash or delicate work. The lines will dry crisp and dense, but large washes are difficult to control and dark areas tend to go patchy.

Cold Pressed (CP or NOT) This paper is sometimes referred to as NOT paper meaning not hot pressed. The surface is semi-rough and textured and is excellent for large washes and line work. It is the most popular choice for the beginner and for many experienced artists.

Rough Paper The coarse surface gives a broken effect to the paint so the results look speckled and the spots of remaining white sparkle. This paper is suitable for bold largescale paintings and is generally used by more experienced artists.

140 gsm

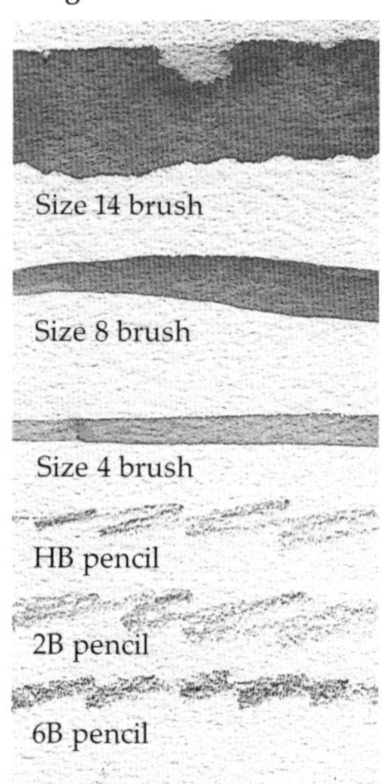

185 gsm

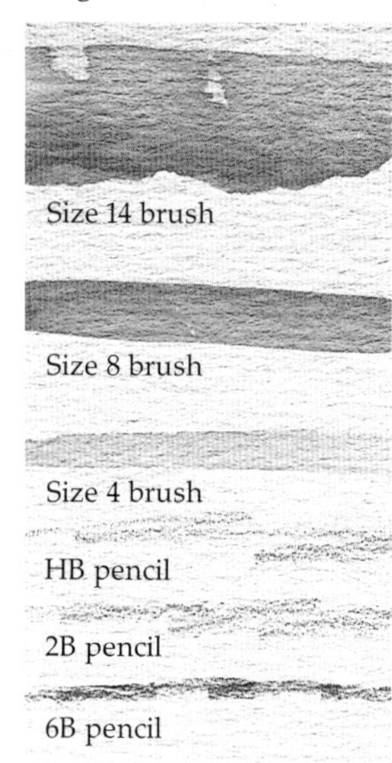

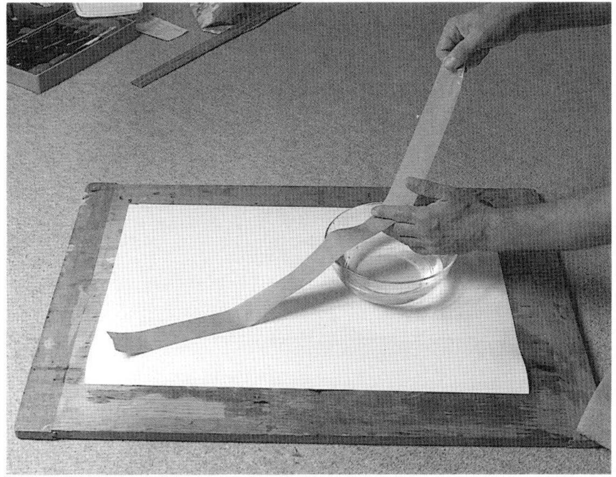

out the centuries. Turner, one of the most creative and innovative of painters, loved good heavy strong paper so he could scrub, cut and scratch into his work. Not for him the Hot Pressed fine smooth surfaces preferred by botanical artists needing to deal with fine line and detail.

Stretching the Paper

The only way to ensure a flat buckle-free surface is to pre-stretch the paper. It is advisable to stretch several sheets at the same time.

1. Use a firm base board of wood (25-30mm) or more thick. Thin plywood or hardboard will warp. Cut the paper to a size approximately 2 inches (50mm) smaller than the board. Cut four strips of 1½ inch (40mm) brown gummed paper strip, two equal to the length and two equal to the height of the board.
2. Sponge the paper on either side, wrong side first, using lukewarm water, which softens the paper slightly more quickly than cold water. Stroke water on to both sides gently so as not to damage the surface and be very careful not to oversaturate the paper. Lay paper on to the board.
3. Press out bubbles with hands, cloth or paper towel, working from the middle to the edges. Wet the strips of gummed tape and run through fingers to remove excess moisture. Place around edges of paper and smooth down with the cloth.
4. Place a tack through each corner. Leave board flat to dry naturally (overnight or several hours). The paper is then ready for use. Paper can be stretched on both sides of a board simultaneously.

Sketchbooks and blocks of watercolor paper are usually made from pre-stretched paper, with the edges glued together. They are unsuitable for use with very wet techniques. Prepared boards, thin watercolor papers mounted on card, are also available.

Equipment

Investing in good quality equipment is money well spent; it is better to buy selectively and have less. Having fewer brushes of finer quality, for example, will encourage you to take time to learn how to use them and to experiment to discover their potential. Good brushes react efficiently and will last a lifetime. Beware of buying kits of brushes or paints; it is usually better to select only the items needed.

Brushes

The best hair brushes are made from red sable. They hold a lot of water and are both soft and springy, with the hairs able to form

300 gsm

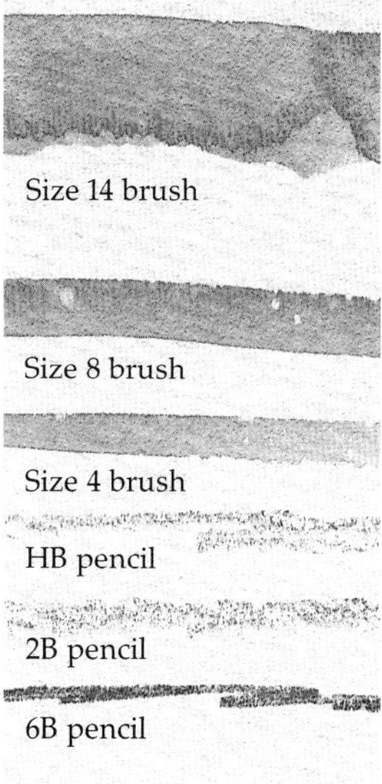

850 gsm

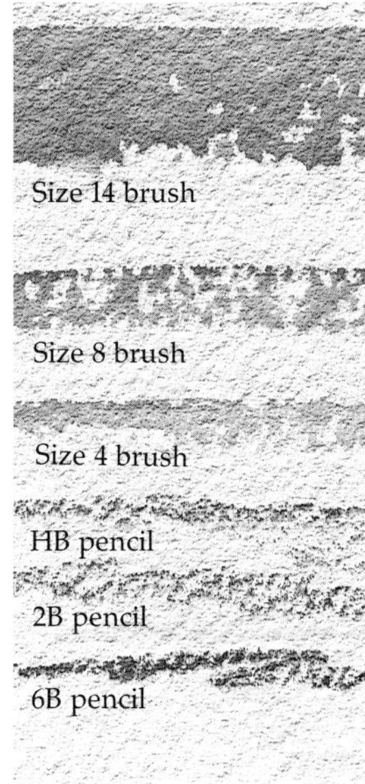

a good point. They are very expensive but will last many years if well treated. Less expensive hair brushes are made from ox hair, which is more springy than sable but holds less water. Camel or squirrel hair brushes are the cheapest. Synthetic brushes can be recommended if they are combined with sable, and are superior to the camel hair brushes. They are usually well priced.

It is unnecessary to buy a wide range of brushes to begin with; initially only two or three are needed. Brushes are graded by size, the smallest being size 000 and the largest size 14. Because watercolor demands large washes and decisive marks, it is better to buy a 4, 8 and 12. Smaller sizes are really only useful for either botanical or highly detailed work. It is also important to relate the size of the brush to the size of the paper; it is a soul-destroying task to work on Half Imperial with small brushes.

Cleaning Brushes Wash brushes in clean water after each session and shape the hairs to a point, or pull the brush backward through thumb and forefinger. If brushes are badly stained, wash them gently in soapy water and rub carefully in the palm of the hand. Rinse them well afterwards and allow to dry naturally, upright in a jar. For longterm storage keep them in a box with moth balls. If a brush gets bent soak it for several hours by laying it in a bowl of water. Shape as before; if necessary wrap a paper tissue around the hairs them allow to dry naturally.

Drawing Board

Drawing boards are vital, and owning several will eventually prove a good long-term investment, as you can use them for stretching paper or have several paintings on the go at one time. There are two kinds, heavyweight for indoor use, either Half Imperial size or Full Imperial depending on preference. For outdoor use a lighter board made from ¼ inch (6mm) plywood is best for a large size of 15x22in (38x56cm); smaller sizes can be a little thinner. There are some good very lightweight timber boards sold by art shops which are fine for smaller sizes, but their disadvantage on a larger scale is they can catch the wind and blow away. Tacks or board clips are necessary to anchor paper.

Easels

Your drawing board can be set either on an easel that has the flexibility to fold back into a range of positions, or on a table easel. Neither is entirely necessary, and a board tilted on a pile of books can be easily substituted. The advantage of an easel such as a metal portable one is that it allows both hands to be free.

Palette

A purpose-made palette has dips or compartments so that large fluid mixes can be kept separate from cakes of paint. A baking tin or large metal or ceramic plate is a useful extra.

Eraser

A soft putty eraser is best for charcoal or very soft pencil and chalk pastel, while an ordinary india rubber is ideal for pencil of all grades. Typewriter or very hard erasers are perfect for removing paint marks and drips from paintings.

Additional Equipment

Masking Fluid and wax crayons or candlewax for protecting white paper.
Gum Arabic for thickening paint.
Glycerine to keep paint moist in hot weather.
Alcohol for cold weather to keep paint (and artist) from freezing.
Water a large bottle plus two containers is essential, one for clean water to use with washes and to mop off errors, and a second for cleaning brushes.
Tapes masking tape for either fastening paper to board or for making straight edges. Brown gummed tape for stretching paper.
Tissue or rags for general corrections and mopping out.
Cotton wool buds and swabs for details or small areas of correction.
Sponges range of sizes for use with paint or water. Also include a large sponge for washes. Natural sponges are better than manufactured.
Knives craft knives or blades for trimming, correcting paint marks or cutting into paper.
Palette knife is useful for applying thick gouache or pigment on to paintings.
Diffuser can be used to blow fine sprays of liquid paint on to work.
Toothbrush for splattering.
Straws to blow liquid paint in controled directions.
Pencils range of grades such as 2B, 4B and 6B; the softest are the most useful.
Charcoal thin and thick sticks.
Wax crayons or pastels good for adding lines of intense color to work; they will cover paler watercolor areas.
Camera useful for quick references to back up working drawings and notes.

When working outside, a good folding stool is a great asset. Make sure it is not too low or heavy; the lightweight aluminum ones are ideal. Some students like to have two so that the palette paints and materials can be rested on the second for easy access. Another option is a three-way canvas chair that packs into a cover with a strap similar to a large umbrella. This can be slung across the shoulders so the body takes its weight, leaving the hands free to carry bags.

Rucksacks or lightweight bags with shoulder straps are best and compartments and pockets useful. Lightweight sleeveless jackets with many large pockets have the advantage that the weight of the paints, sketchbooks and other equipment is spread across the body and the hands are free. If the subject matter demands a long walk or hike, a jacket is a sensible purchase.

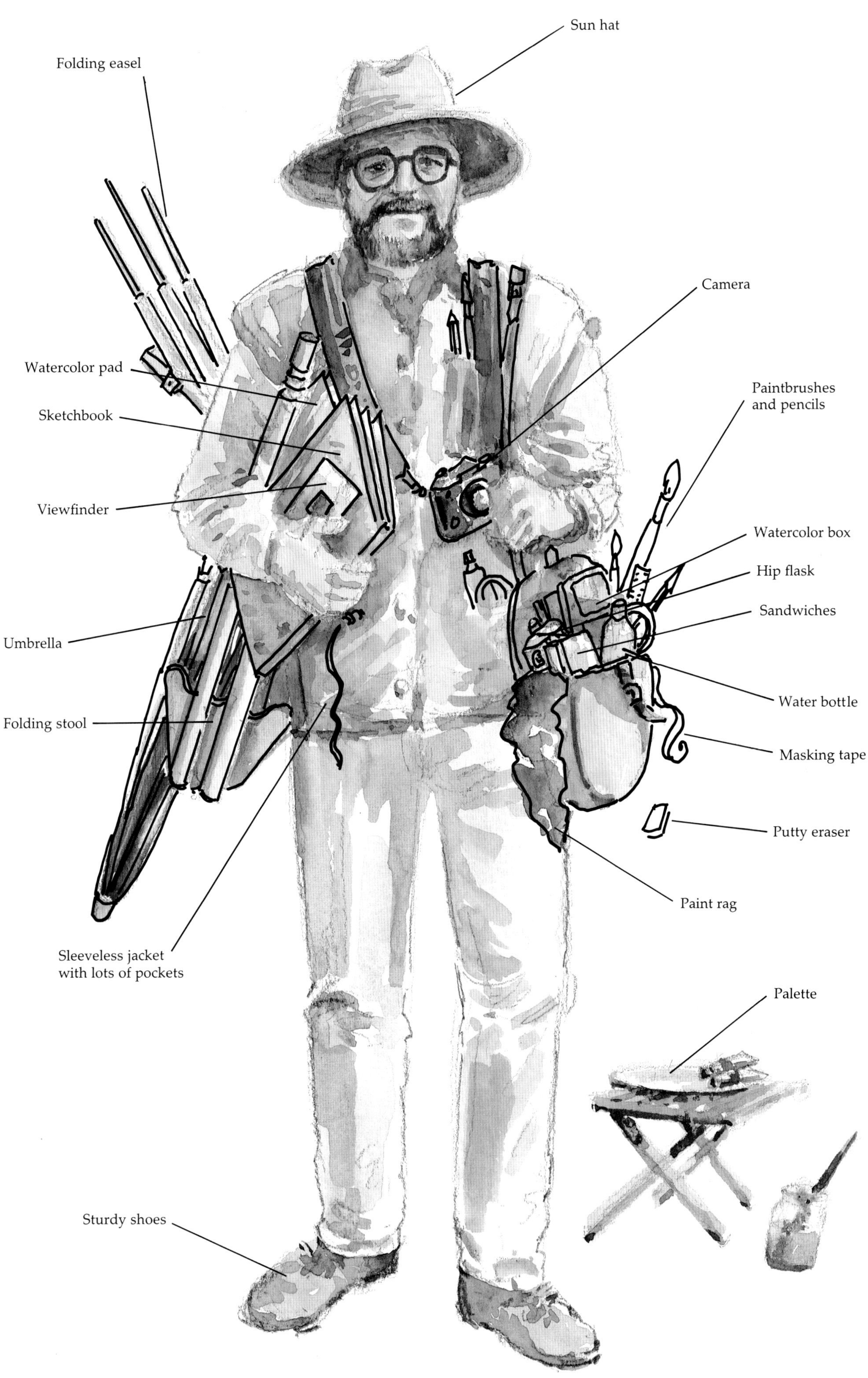
Sun hat
Folding easel
Camera
Watercolor pad
Paintbrushes and pencils
Sketchbook
Viewfinder
Watercolor box
Hip flask
Sandwiches
Umbrella
Water bottle
Folding stool
Masking tape
Putty eraser
Paint rag
Sleeveless jacket with lots of pockets
Palette
Sturdy shoes

LEFT
Kevin Chapman
The Temperate House, Kew
Watercolor and gouache, 9½×13½ inches (24.3×34.6cm)
This atmospheric painting is a good introduction to watercolor; the artist has used the pure form of the medium to lay in the luminous washes, with plenty of water and big bold brush marks. The detail is worked in layers over these, using selective marks and richer colors. The fine detail was added last, with small brushes and accents of color or darker tones. As a result the spontaneous moody background complements the architectural detail of the conservatory.

Paints

The term watercolor can either be used specifically to describe a range of translucent paints or it can be used more broadly to include a whole range of water-based paints. These will include watercolor, gouache, poster paints, indian inks, acrylics and tempera. Because they are all water-based they can be used either together on a painting or individually. It is therefore important briefly to describe them and their basic properties.

Watercolor

In its pure sense watercolor refers to a translucent medium used without white. Lighter tones are obtained not by adding white pigment but by thinning with water so that light is created by the paper showing through the thinner layer of paint. The method of using it in washes on white paper gives the paint great luminosity and in this pure form was developed primarily by the English watercolorists in the eighteenth century. The pigments were diluted with water giving rise to the term 'wash'. If white is added then the paints lose their transparency. If white is mixed into the pigment the paint is then called 'gouache'.

Pure watercolor is available in several forms, dry cakes, semi-moist pans, tubes and bottles of concentrated color.

Dry Cakes These contain pigment in its purest form and are the traditional form of watercolor. The cakes need plenty of water to release the color and, unless used regularly, will get very hard and will need to be well worked with water before use. Cheap tins of cake paints are sold as children's or amateur sets. If they are totally submersed in clean water for half an hour and then drained before use, they become much softer and easier to use. One of the main drawbacks of hard cakes is the difficulty of taking on substantial amounts of

BELOW
Rosemary Williams
Welsh Hills
Colored inks on paper,
The luminosity of color in this Welsh landscape is created by thin overlayers of diluted permanent inks. Their advantage over pure watercolor is that they dry quickly and so layers of color can be built up independently as they will not intermix. This gives a rich glow to the color. Once dry, the colors are fixed and can only be changed by overpainting with an opaque medium such as gouache or acrylic.

color, so that it appears saturated when used.

Pans and Half Pans These are small semi-moist blocks designed to fit into metal water-color boxes. They can be bought separately so each artist can make his own color choices. It is easy to work off more saturated color, and also easier to control the dilution of the color with water. Pans are convenient for outdoor use, being portable and flexible.

Tubes These are ideal if paint is needed in large quantities or for larger scale paintings. They will dry out on the palette fairly quickly but can be kept moist by adding glycerine, honey or sugar.

Bottled Watercolor Bottled watercolors are intense; the bottles usually come complete with a dropper for depositing the paint on to a palette. Use sparingly as they will dry fairly quickly on to the palette.

Quality Manufacturers grade their paint according to quality and durability. Artist's quality is the best and most expensive. Student's quality is more fugitive; color will fade more quickly but they may be up to one quarter of the price of the artist's range.

Gouache

Gouache or body color is an opaque water-color, and the pigments are not so finely ground. Its binding agent is gum arabic and, more recently, plastic. The pigment has white added to it which makes the paint opaque, losing the translucency of pure watercolor. This does mean that light can be laid over darks, and the picture can be built up with solid color. As a medium gouache offers more flexibility than pure watercolor, allowing the layering of dark, light, then dark, so that detail and complex images can be developed.

The medium is extensively used by commercial artists and illustrators, the opacity of the paint allowing flat even areas of color to be painted. The strength and saturation of color is excellent for graphic reproduction. The range of paints for commercial use are labeled 'Designer's Colors'.

Gouache ranges are sold in tubes or bottles. Poster paints are a cheaper and less reliable version frequently used by schools and art students.

ABOVE
Antonia Black
Crescent over Konya
Gouache on paper, 22¼×30 inches (60×76.8cm)
This lively and colorful painting is made up of thick and thin layers of gouache laid on to the picture with large brushes. The large areas of light color are painted in first with watery paint and then allowed to dry before the rich detail is added later. Maximum opacity is retained when little water, if any, is added to the paint.

ABOVE
Hazel Penwarden
Autumn Fruits
Indian ink and pen on paper, 11½×16¼ inches (29.4×41.6cm)
This is a finely drawn and detailed study, made in pen with indian ink. The texture and tones have all been built up with careful marks that express the structure and character of the fruits and leaves. The whole process is slow and demanding and any mistakes cannot be eliminated, only absorbed back into the overall drawing. As a technique, it is useful for a beginner to explore because it demands clarity of vision coupled with decision and careful control of each line.

Inks

This medium has been used for over 2000 years, pens being made from quills, bronze and finally steel. Currently available are dip pens, fountain pens – for use with non-waterproof inks – and reservoir pens for graphics use and with waterproof ink.

Artist's quality inks are waterproof and translucent and can be thinned with water. When dry they can receive more layers on top, the resulting colors being rich and luxurious. Indian ink is a black waterproof drawing ink which can be diluted with water. Non-waterproof inks sink into the paper more than the waterproof and have a matt finish. Good quality heavy cartridge paper is ideal for inks and will take a wash. The lines will remain crisp. Paper should be stretched if large washes are to be used.

Using line and wash is an excellent discipline to develop both drawing skills and an understanding of tone and will increase your confidence and spontaneity. Experimenting with just one color and a dip pen or quill will not be expensive, yet offers experience of making decisive and direct statements.

Acrylics

The pigments are bound in a synthetic resin, either an actual acrylic or PVA (polyvinyl acetate). The medium is either soluble in water, or thinned with more PVA, or a mixture of both. Acrylics are extremely versatile and can be used in translucent washes and overlays or as thick opaque unipasto similar to an oil paint. They dry very quickly and until now seemed very durable. It is only recently that doubts have been cast about their permanence, as well known and valuable examples have started to deteriorate in public collections.

They were increasingly popular from the 1950s and were used by painters such as Rothko, Motherwell, Noland, Hockney and Barnett Newman, who worked on a huge scale. They can be used on a wide range of surfaces from papers through to canvas, wood, hardboard and strawboard, none of which need a primer although one is normally used. It is best to stretch papers if large washes are to be used.

Brushes for acrylic are usually the same as for oil paints, but the paint has one major disadvantage that it drys very quickly, so care must be taken to keep brushes moist at all times. The specially designed 'wet palette' is useful to keep paint moist as it lies on the palette as the paints will dry quickly.

FAR LEFT BELOW
Elaine Anderson
Costume Design for Carmina Burana
Colored inks, 11½×9 inches (29.4×23cm)
Inks can be used in a very free way as both lines and washes. They are an ideal medium for a designer, as demonstrated by this spontaneous costume design. The artist has used a pen and two or three brush sizes for the line work, while some of the detail suggesting texture in the dress has been diluted with water.

LEFT
Liz Knutt
Summer Bouquet
Acrylic and oil pastel on paper,
Acrylic paints can be used on any surface, from paper to wood or metal; in this example the artist has used a textured watercolor paper. The paints were first used as atmospheric background color by diluting them with water and applying them freely with a large brush. The flowers were then overpainted in thick swirls to suggest their form. Detail was either added in paint with smaller brushes or drawn in using an oil-based pastel. These are best used over water-based paints; if used under them they may well crack and flake off, as oil and water will not mix. The result is a fresh delicate painting which is full of rich color and some fine drawing.

3. Basic Techniques

Techniques evolve in any medium firstly through exploring its innate qualities, secondly through looking at examples from the past, and finally through the need to express personal ideas. The most successful exponents in any medium are also great practitioners of the craft.

Historically the greatest painters began their careers as assistants, where they could first learn to practice the rules thoroughly before breaking them in their quest to express personal ideas. Tracing the transition from masters' techniques through to students' innovations is a fascinating and enlightening method of learning. Modern artists are at an advantage in that such a wealth of work is readily accessible both through museums and galleries and through sophisticated reproduction techniques.

Most artists will experience their introduction to painting and drawing as children, when they will explore bright colors and cheap water-based paints. Teachers anxious to stimulate self-expression will encourage their pupils to revel in new media through play and experiments. Even as an adult it will be beneficial to begin with a similar exploratory session. The hardest moment for many artists, let alone the beginner, is putting down the first mark, so for basic exercises using cheap paper is an advantage. The first objective is to play and doodle with the pencil or paint to see how many configurations, marks and patterns can be made. Paint can be applied very wet or dry, water added before and after. Even at such a simple level each student will produce marks personal to them, in the way handwriting becomes unique to the individual. This is one of the most important exercises for everyone to try because you can enjoy using the medium freely and not be inhibited by lack of drawing or painting skills. The results will suggest many ideas for further use and development.

As already discussed (page 16), the term watercolor can be used to mean both pure watercolor and any paint ground up in a water-soluble medium, including gouache, tempera, ink and acrylic. Two primary techniques are the basis for all watercolor media: how to lay on a flat wash, and how to manipulate and control the brush.

LEFT
Anita Young
Abstract Watercolor
Watercolor, 13×20¼ inches (33×52cm)
The vigor and contrast and the scale of the paint marks are here complementary to each other. A large decorator's brush has been used to paint the bold sweeps of the background. When this was dry the controlled and rhythmic foreground marks were made 'from the shoulder', so that they glide across the surface, subdividing the space.

The inspiration for this picture came from two sources. Firstly the artist explored the mark-making qualities of the medium and examined their potential. Secondly, she had made a number of earlier drawings about the landscape, divided by patterns or hedges and roads. These divisions fascinated her and inspired many subsequent paintings which slowly became more abstract, so that the subject of the painting became the division of space, rather than the realistic interpretation of a landscape.

LEFT
Paul Klee (1879-1940)
Three Houses, 1922
Watercolor on laid paper bordered by violet watercolor mounted on light cardboard, 7⅞×11⅞ inches (20×30.2cm), Metropolitan Museum, New York, Berggreuen Klee collection
Paul Klee made many hundreds of paintings in watercolor, often based on a grid, yet each was innovative and evocative, utilizing the many simple techniques of washes, layered washes and simple controled marks made with a brush.

Flat Wash

This is the foundation for all pure watercolor which needs to be laid across any area too big for one brush stroke. The aim is to lay the paint down on the paper so it looks totally flat and consistent, showing no uneveness or variation in tone.

The paper should be stretched (for instructions on how to do this, see page 13) and the drawing board placed at a slight angle so that the paint and water can run slowly down the paper. The secret of a flat wash is in using plenty of water. First dampen the paper in the area where the wash is to be painted. Mix up plenty of paint, a wash

Antonia Black
Camel Tenders in Tunisia
Watercolor, 9×12 inches (23×30cm)
This lovely simple painting was made quickly in a sketchbook. It is composed of three types of wash with detail laid on the top of them. The sky is a wet wash of pale diluted color painted on to damp paper. The sketchbook was held at a slight angle so that the color could run down the paper. Next the line of trees was painted and some of their color has run into the sky; this gives a sensation of hazy heat, so this 'accident' is beneficial to the painting. The beach was probably painted next, with thin watery paint and limited pigment. This was followed by adding the details of camels and their attendants. The color has run a little into the sand, creating a good shadow. Next, when everything was dry, the sea was painted with a strong intense dark blue, so the color of the sea is overprinted. The result is fresh and atmospheric, the methods used simple. The observation and selection of how and what to paint has been developed throughout a large number of washes.

takes up an unexpectedly large amount, then fully load the brush. Use a very large size watercolor brush; a decorator's brush or sponges are also excellent. Apply the paint swiftly in a relaxed and rhythmic manner starting at the top of the paper, then working across from left to right, then from right to left, allowing no spaces between the sweeps. Gravity will aid the flow, and the marks will all blend in together. Leave the board flat to dry; if a damp wash is painted into, clean edges will run and this forms the basis of WET INTO WET. Because watercolor is transparent the white paper will glow through the color. The more water that is added to the paint the lighter it will appear. Watercolors usually change color when they dry, appearing lighter in tone.

Graduated Wash

This is a development from the flat wash. As the paint is applied across and down the

David Wise
Still Life with Fruit and Flowers
Watercolor, 29¾×22 inches (76×56.3cm)
The title of this painting could also be *Composition of Sphere and Circles,* for these shapes are central to both the subjects and the background. Each object develops the form through color, pattern and technique. The flowers are outlines with an undulating and rhythmic line which creates a powerful pattern. This shape is echoed more softly through a series of round washes with edges of intense color made through backruns, which creates a background foil to the flowers. The ellipses of the vase and plate move the eye down to the fruit sitting solidly at the table. Finally, the strong red linear shadows complete and hold the bottom of the composition together.

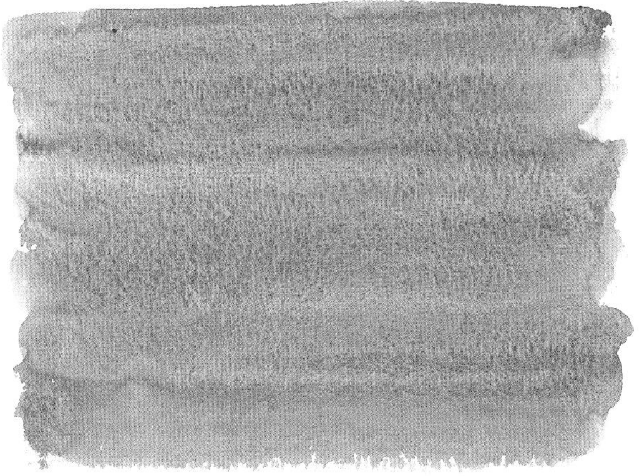

FAR LEFT
Flat wet wash

LEFT
Variegated wash
Red through to blue.

FAR LEFT BELOW
Graduated wash

LEFT BELOW
Tonal layers
Showing the five tones of blue made with overlays of the same paint mixture. These washes are the foundation of all watercolor technique and can be identified constantly in artists' works. It is worth practicing them as simple washes on a small scale, then repeating them in larger, more complex proportions. Different papers will react in new ways, so trial and error on a small sample is sensible when exploring new media. It is a mistake always to use the same combination of materials; results and skills will quickly become jaded and slick. New materials offer new challenges and will always help to extend your ability. All these techniques and methods apply to the whole range of water-based media, including acrylics.

paper, more and more clean water is added to each sweep so that the pigment is increasingly diluted.

Variegated Wash

The colors must be mixed in advance and then applied speedily. The paper needs predamping. One color is applied to the top and allowed to run down. The second color is then painted across the bottom so that both washes run and blend into each other. Once blended the board is left flat to dry.

Tones

Tonal values can be built up using the same color, by first allowing the paint or wash to dry then adding new layers of paint. Each layer must be dry before adding the next. The more layers that are added the darker the tone becomes. Colors laid on top of each other will show color changes because of the translucency of the paint, so a red over a yellow will show as an orange.

Backruns

These are the result of working on to a wash before it has properly dried. This accidental effect can be developed and used by the more experienced artist.

Wet on to Dry Paper

The essence of this wash is the unevenness of the color against the areas of white paper that remain. The wash is applied directly to dry paper with a brush that is not overloaded with paint. When it is dragged across the surface it leaves the rough texture of the paper standing proud. This adds a sparkle to the picture, and the paint is crisper and more controlable than with a wet wash.

Dry washes can be used alone or over earlier different colored wet washes. The results can be very expressive.

Granulated Washes

Certain pigments seem to separate in water so they cause a speckled effect which can add a subtle texture and atmosphere. They work well across other washes; the colors to experiment with are cerulean and ultramarine blues, burnt and raw umbers and yellow ocher. The results are not predictable and will vary according to the manufacturer.

Problems

You can give yourself problems if you fail to mix enough paint at the outset, use insufficient water, tip the board too much so that the paint runs too fast or fail to ensure that the first wash is dry. Qualities created accidentally can, however, frequently be very innovative and exciting. Sometimes they can be left or they may be developed by further work or addition of other techniques. This is how techniques and ideas occur – but a period of time for thought and contemplation prior to action or remedy is advisable.

Brush Control

Learning how to control the brushes needs thought and practice. Just as a musician regularly practices musical scales, learning to paint needs a similar attitude, and the discipline of exploring brush control will help confidence, flexibility and control. Five or ten minutes limbering up on a regular basis with pencils as well as paint is time well invested.

This painting of *Simonside* in Northumberland (far right) is deceptively simple, based on a composition of half sky and half land. Each summarizes both the essence of Northumberland and the power of basic watercolor techniques, the simple washes and decisive brush marks. Added to this is an understanding of the theories and rules of perspective and color, utilized to create a sensation of three-dimensional paper. These have been learned and absorbed, through practice, by the artist, so that the painting was made intuitively but guided by logic. The result is fresh and spontaneous, and the artist's intentions (what she wanted to say) are made very clear.

Composition. This is based on horizontal subdivisions running parallel across the sky and background. The space between them diminishes as they reach the focal point of the distant hills. This perspective device creates a sense of space and depth in the sky. The eye is led into the picture through several gentle diagonals of the foreground grasses are made in the opposite direction to being the eye back into the picture.

Color. Warm colors such as reds will come forward, while cool colors such as blues will recede. The artist has made full use of this fact by painting the foreground in rich warm red/browns, which become cooler and more purple with the addition of blue. The background is cool pale blue/grays. The sky has cool lemon yellows in the background and warmer blue/grays overhead.

Tone. There are four combinations of large tones into which any landscape can be organized to give a suggestion of depth and recession to both the land and the sky. The foreground can either be painted with a broad graduated wash from dark through to light at the horizon, or vice versa. The sky can be treated similarly, from dark overhead to light at the horizon or vice versa. This gives four possibilities as the basis for the pictorial space into which the objects, clouds, trees, buildings and roads are placed. The Simonside hills have the dark (overhead) graduating to light (background) for the sky and light (foreground) graduating to dark (background) for the land.

Techniques. The sky is painted with a wet into wet variegated wash. The yellow band for the background was painted first, with the board rotated so that it could run. Next the board was returned to its normal position and the larger gray wash laid in using large brushes. The darker bands of clouds fed into the damp underwash and the board was then tilted, allowing gravity to ease the wash down the paper to intermingle with the yellow. The land was also painted with further washes. The details of the grasses were painted with two different size brushes so the scale of marks changed accordingly, resulting in the suggestion of more space created by the large marks against the small.

BELOW
Elaine Alderson
Plant in a Pot
Watercolor, 16½×11 inches (42.2×28.1cm)
This exercise, painted in a limited number of colors, is a series of controled but very simple brush marks laid on to dry paper. The light areas are painted in first, using thin watery paint; this defines the basic shape and structure of the plant. Further layers of paint are added, with each being allowed to dry before adding the next. The overpainting creates a new range of tones and colors, besides clarifying more detail of the plant.

LEFT
Elaine Alderson
Simonside
Watercolor, 15×22 inches (38.4×56.3cm)

Brushstrokes in sizes

14

8

4

6B pencil

Size 4, 14 brushes

Exercises

This is a list of simple exercises that can be modified or added to as is necessary. Try them with a full range of brushes, pencils and pens. Always ensure that the brush is well loaded with paint.

1. Make horizontal lines left to right keeping an even pressure.

Hold the brush at different angles and repeat the above.

Vary the direction of brush marks by turning the brush at right angles to make a controlled corner.

2 Repeat all the above exercises using dry paint.

3. Experiment with random brush movements using first the wrist, then the forearm, then from the shoulder. Use wet and dry paint.

4. Paint a solid circle in one light sweep.

Paint a solid triangle in three tight sweeps.

Paint a solid square in three or four sweeps. Keep the corners controled.

5. Make lots of parallel lines, trying to keep them similar in weight and strength.

6. Make lots of parallel lines, varying the pressure; first heavy at the beginning and light at the end of each mark, then reverse this to light at the beginning and heavy at the end of each mark.

7. Take a line for a 'walk' around the paper, first with even pressure, then vary the pressure. See how long the line is before you run out of paint.

8. Lightly draw a simple geometric pattern, then experiment with painting each area with a different technique. Try to not paint over the edges. This can be painted first in one color then in several colors.

BELOW LEFT AND RIGHT
These six illustrations have been selected from many more all of which experiment with making marks using pen, brush, chalk or string, each being applied using different gestures and rhythm. The results form the nucleus of the visual language to be developed later into a means of expressing pictorial ideas (see page 28).

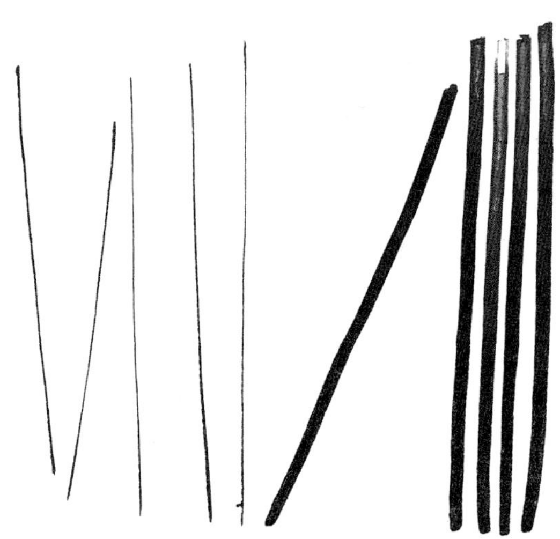

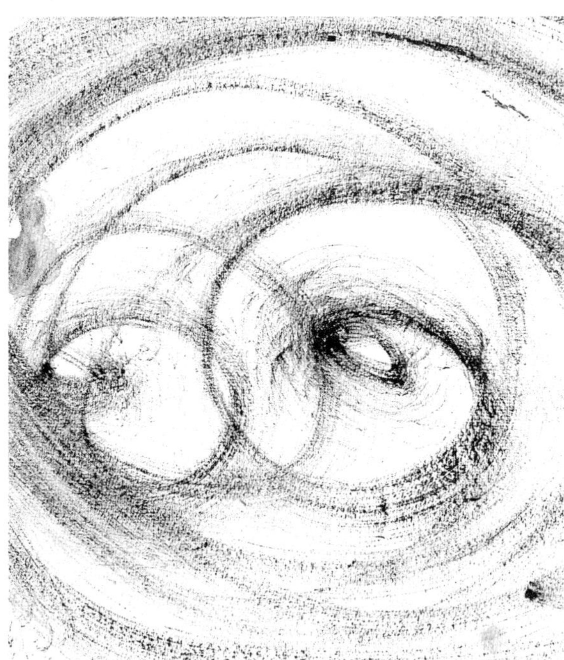

Kevin Chapman
Riverside I
Mixed media, watercolor, gouache and inks, 9¾×13½ inches (25×34.6cm)
This bold sweeping painting encompasses the rhythms and linear qualities of the tree using a range of mixed media and marks. The broad shapes were laid in first, followed by the detail of the branches. The interpretation is not realistic because the artist has exaggerated movement and pattern, which has been expressively painted and drawn showing real enjoyment of the scene.

Development of a Visual Language

The goal for every artist should be to develop an individual approach to their work, through which intentions and priorities are communicated. This process takes time and plenty of practice, The artist has to learn how to look at an analysis of his results as well as at the subject. Many beginners confuse techniques with intention and expend more energy on the former. It is the intention of the painting that is the key to deciding what is the priority of the subject. The most exciting and rewarding paintings are frequently very simple in their content, color, composition or technique – but if all these elements are brought together deliberately and succinctly, the ideas will be communicated more powerfully.

Each time an artist makes a painting or drawing, new ideas are formulated and crystallized which are developed further in the subsequent works. There may be suggestions for new color relationships, or exploring space or form. The subject may benefit from another viewpoint or a restructuring of the composition. Each artist develops an individual language of marks, symbols, devices and priorities, for example pattern, atmosphere or color.

The illustration of simple marks made with layers of washes can be copied by a total beginner. When the results are looked at, they start suggesting simple images, such as a row of books lined up on a shelf, or a pattern on a rug or fabric, or perhaps they evoke a wooden fence. A very simple technique can be the basis of a painting.

David Wise is fascinated by the fences, patterns and simple geometric structures found all around him in his immediate neighborhood. He finds the Victorian suburbs of London an endless source of inspiration. This is coupled with his love of heightened (bright) color, and bold decisive watercolor used with large brushes and plenty of water.

The painting entitled *Washing* was made on location. The composition is simple, relying on a structure formed by the horizontals of the houses, set against the gradual diagonals of the fences and the washing

LEFT
David Wise
Preliminary sketch for Washing
Pencil, 21½×14½ inches (55×37.1cm)

BELOW
Simple exercises in layering paint and practicing brush control can be developed into more complex compositions such as those of David Wise opposite.

line. The key lines of the subject are probably intuitively related to the harmony set out by the golden section (see page 59) which means they are placed in a ratio of roughly one third to two thirds across the paper. The large shapes are painted with a wet wash on to dry paper. The resulting unevenness gives texture and subtlety to such a large simple area. The fence is boldly painted with strong decisive paint marks, using plenty of watery paint (they are similar in their direct approach to the marks of the first exercise). By using a range of intense colors, the panels of a very ordinary wooden fence are vitalized and establish a strong foreground. The color scheme is the main force of the picture, and is based on two sets of complementary colors, yellows and their opposite violets, and reds and their opposite greens (see page 51). These color combinations energize each other and also let the eye move across the surface of the picture as it looks for them. This increases the animation of the fluttering washing. Thus a simple everyday subject which could have easily been overlooked becomes the stimulus for a painting, and through the interpretation of the artist is transformed into a visually exciting image.

The idea is developed further by the artist looking critically at his result, then looking for further subject matter. The first step was to change the viewpoint, so instead of working from the back of the houses, he moved around to the front. He has also changed the paper from the horizontal (landscape) position to a vertical (portrait) position. Next a drawing is made concentrating on the structure, pattern and composition; no attempt is made to show tone or volume, because it is of no interest to this artist. His intention is to organize the geometric shapes of the buildings against the organic verticals of the trees. He uses selected branches to help lead the eye into and around the space. The painting made from the drawing is worked on in the studio, the drawing and *Washing* giving enough ideas and information to be put together into a new painting. The composition is guided by information gathered in the drawing. The color is intense and an interplay developed between the background (negative image) and the foreground (the positive image). The result is an abstract mosaic of jewel-like colors which fuse and interrelate with the subject. The houses and trees are either revealed or concealed through the structure and color relationships in the picture. This conflicting information sets up visual tensions which hold the attention of the viewer.

The series of pictures and drawings made by the artist demonstrate how ordinary subjects can be developed simply but powerfully, when the artist is clear about his intentions and confident about his areas of particular interest.

ABOVE
David Wise
Washing
Watercolor, 21×18½ inches
(53.8×47.4cm)

BELOW
David Wise
Houses at St Margarets
Watercolor, 22×22 inches
(56.3×56.3cm)

4. Drawing

Drawings are made for three very broad reasons. Firstly as a discipline; since about 1400 Western man has regarded drawing as the foundation to his art, whether he be a painter or cabinet maker. Secondly it is a means of communicating ideas and thoughts. Finally it can be a tool for conveying information, such as the map to the London Underground service.

Learning to draw is one of the most important jobs an artist can accomplish. The process is very similar to learning a new language, where a few simple words will immediately open up new and rewarding channels of communication, which in turn can be extended by learning more vocabulary, and developing and understanding the theory and structure of the language. The

LEFT
Leonardo da Vinci
Study for the Kneeling Leda, c.1504
Pen, bister and wash over black chalk, 6¼×5½ inches (16×13.9cm)
Devonshire Collection, Chatsworth House, Derbyshire, reproduced by permission of the Trustees of the Chatsworth Settlement.
'Consider with the greatest diligence the boundaries of anybody and the manner of their serpentine turning. This serpentine turning must be inspected to see whether its sides partake of rounded curvature or of angular concavity' – Leonardo da Vinci. This voluptuous Leda is drawn with fine confident pen work that expresses the volume of the figure while at the same time giving it life and energy with every stroke. The subject is a celebration of birth and nature.

verbal symbols can be used by all ability levels to express individual ideas and needs.

The language of drawing is based on the development of marks or symbols which relate to specific objects in the surrounding environment. The artist needs to refer continually from the drawing to the subject throughout the time needed to make the drawing. The repeated process of looking and then recording gives a deep and concentrated insight into both the subject and the artist's imagination or thought process. Improved drawing skills help the ability to paint, with the added bonus that more complex subjects can be tackled with increasing confidence.

One point to bear in mind is that drawing is a far more widely ranging skill than at first appears and does not imply just pencil and line. Leonardo's *Study for the Kneeling Leda* (left) consists mainly of outlines, while giving full value to the volume of the figure, but in Seurat's *Seated Boy* (page 34) the linear construction of the drawing is much less clear, and Degas used pastel for some drawings.

How to Draw

All artists have a visual curiosity about their environment, and for many this will be the sole concern throughout their working life. Others will use the information they acquire to enrich their imagination, and develop their memory and observation skills. The ability to observe and then record information accurately is vital to every artist at some stage in their development. Most people when they first begin to draw will record *what they know* rather than *what they see*.

To fully appreciate how bad most people's observation is, try making a drawing of an object from memory, after studying the object for some minutes. It is frightening to see how quickly the memory fades leaving the drawing incomplete. If this exercise is repeated frequently, however, the capacity of the memory expands. Relevant information about the subject is selected and stored, resulting in fuller more complete drawings, conveying information about the proportion, perspective, volume and texture of the subject and not just superficial narrative detail. There are many exercises which can help the artist to visualize via a drawing what is seen. It is helpful to practice each exercise independently, and also at its most basic level; the information will seem less confusing and easier to absorb.

ABOVE
Auguste Rodin (1840-1917)
Kneeling Girl
Drawing, graphite with watercolor on white paper, laid down, 12¾×9½ inches (32.6×24.7cm)
Art Institute of Chicago, Alfred Stieglitz Collection (1949.895)

LEFT
Foundation Study: Standing Figure
Charcoal on paper,
The distribution of weight and the stance of this pose is drawn with economical and concentrated lines in charcoal. The emphasis of the drawing is on the counterbalance between the upward movement of the stretched arms and the distribution of weight through the torso and legs to the floor. The central strength and curvature of the spine is suggested through the thrust and fullness of the stomach.

Measured Drawing

This is a key exercise and will enable you to paint or draw to scale and with the objects in correct proportion to each other.

You should choose a fixed viewpoint, and a position not too close to the subject. Select a range of about 45° which is within the field of vision; objects either side of this will become distorted or out of focus. Do not move your head while looking at the subject. Use your pencil as a measuring device, holding it out horizontally or vertically at arm's length, with one eye closed. Align the top of the pencil with the top of a chosen object, and move the thumb down the pencil until it coincides with the bottom. This is the key measure, and it can be related up and down and across the subject so the size of one area can be compared with the next. A mark can be put on the paper for reference at each measured point. Thus a cereal pack can be drawn to scale with a box of tea or one building drawn to scale with another.

If the key measures are translated directly to the paper, the drawing made will be exactly the same as it is seen so it will be a sight-sized drawing. If the scale of the drawing needs to be bigger, the key measure will need to be transposed into a bigger scale on the drawing.

This method initially results in rather 'wooden' drawings and is quite tiring, but with practice the process speeds up and can be used in conjunction with free drawing as well as linear perspective.

Relationship of Diagonals to the Horizontals and Verticals

Simple assessments can be made as to the general accuracy of diverging lines on a page by using the pencil or brush as a visual guide. This is held out vertically or horizontally at arm's length. The subject is examined against the line, and you can easily see if the line of the building follows it or whether a line diverges away. Should this happen, the angle between the two can be assessed and the simple rules of perspective applied (see page 38).

The observation can be transferred to the paper by either lightly pulling in the vertical or horizontal or laying the pencil along a similar position. The angles can then be easily assessed; it is surprising how frequently diverging lines are misinterpreted.

When the diverging lines of a diminishing subject need to be checked and rectified, a pencil, long straight stick or ruler can be held in alignment with them. The line can then be followed through until it meets the vanishing point on the horizon line (see page 39).

Tone, Shape and Form

A shape can be both positive and negative. This relationship is important for giving an impression of space, solidity or three-dimensionality to the work. How the shape is recorded will also alter its value; a line drawing in pencil will give quite a different interpretation to one in charcoal or watercolor.

Line used alone can create ambiguity, but when used with tone, the form can be clarified. Tone is the graduation from light to dark in either monochrome or color. The lightest area is created by light falling on to the subject; without tone, objects disappear into the background. A white shape will only be visible on white paper if it is set against a dark background. The lightest area in the work can be either the white of the paper or paint.

To make them look bright and light on the drawing or painting, the background tonal values may need adjusting accordingly, even if in reality tones may seem to be close. The maximum illusion of depth will be achieved by fully developing the whole tonal range of each medium. When using color, note that each one has a value relative to a monochrome tonal scale from white through a range of halftones (grays) to black. For instance the yellows will relate to lighter halftones than the blues.

The method of applying the medium also accentuates the appearance of solidity of the form. Relating the marks made by the pencil or brush to the contours of the form will help to describe the volume. The marks can either be applied directly and left, or blended into one another subtly. Whatever the chosen medium, the subject and its background must be carefully analysed, in order to evaluate the shape, size and direction of each light and dark. The most common mistake the beginner makes is to record tones in isolation from each other.

The first priority is to simplify the subject into the largest lights and darks; whether they fall on the object or the background. This can be achieved by either half closing the eyes, or by thinking of the subject emerging from a thick fog which slowly clears. The largest darks or lights can then be deciphered and recorded before breaking

FAR LEFT
Rosemary Williams
Quenton Crisp
Pencil on paper, 19½×11 inches (49.9×28.2 cm)
Exploring the structure of a nude figure is a way of developing an understanding of its volume and three dimensionality. In this drawing the center of gravity through the figure is well established and the contraposto stance emphasized as a means to the careful analysis and understanding of the inner structure and anatomy. Although this is a linear drawing, volume and the solidity of the form are powerfully expressed by identifying the cross-sections which establish and denote the changes of plane and volume.

BELOW
This pencil study by Elaine Alderson shows how one object found within the subject can be used as a key measure. Once established, this can then be related to other objects and areas of the drawing so that they can be drawn proportionally to this key.

them down into smaller halftones. The fact that tones appear to run together and do not exist solely on the object or background helps to create exciting ambiguities. Coupled with this, the brain can get confused when the eye tries to read the balance between negative and positive shapes. This light/dark balance has important potential energy value in a painting or drawing.

Exercises

There are several useful exercises which can be tackled in a range of media to develop a practical awareness of the positive and negative relationships of shape and form.

1. First make a series of studies of a simple object and background, trying to find different ways to show the form. Use a range of media including paint and drawing media plus different backgrounds – dark and light. When comparing the results look for the methods which really show the volume of the object.
2. Secondly, using either charcoal and an eraser or one color and white, make a study of another simple object and background lit with a strong light. The aim is to use dark shapes against light to find the edges. Put down the broad simple dark shapes, and correct them by using the eraser or white paint to find the proportion, and edge of the dark, as one meets the other. When the large forms are found and proportionally correct, then smaller halftones can be added. Try not to use any lines at all, as the temptation is to just fill them in, rather than develop an ability to manipulate one against another.

Seurat is a master of this technique, and even his simplest drawings show a mastery of chiaroscuro – the balance of light and shadow and atmosphere. He went on to develop his use of color and paint in a similar way by clearly distinguishing one from another.

What to draw

The beginner needs to spend some time in practicing how to draw, to understand the scale and relationship of objects, and how to measure them up and correct their proportions. The development of volume and form through using tone will take time to master. The next step is to decide what are the aims of the drawing – a clear intention will help suggest methods and approach. No one drawing can contain all the elements equally emphasized; the priorities and selection are the prerogative of each artist. The most important point to remember is that the draw-

LEFT
Georges Seurat (1859-91)
Seated Boy with Straw Hat, 1882
Conté crayon drawing, 9½×12¼ inches (24.3×31.4cm)
Yale University Art Gallery, Everett V. Meeks, BA 1901 Fund
This beautiful study was used in the final painting of *The Swimmers*, 1883-84, which was planned through many meticulous drawings and paintings. This drawing sums up Seurat's philosophy, which was explained so well by his friend Paul Signac in the *Revue Blanche*: 'Seurat's studies resulted in his well considered and fertile theory of contrasts: a theory to which all his work was thereafter subjected. He applied it first to chiaroscuro: with the simplest of resources, the white sheet of paper and black conté crayon skilfully graded or contrasted, he executed some four hundred drawings, the most beautiful painters' drawings in existence. And then, having achieved mastery of contrasts of tone, he tackled color in the same way.

Rita Hodson
Still Life with Leaves.
This artist has harnessed the ambiguous, alternating balance between the form (positive shapes) and the background (negative shapes). This results in a dynamic energy created between them, caused by the visual confusion, that never seems to be resolved.

ing should be as individual to each artist as is their handwriting.

Drawing is a valuable method of enquiry into the natural world, which involves focusing attention and expressing feeling, whether it be a subjective (from the heart) or objective (from the head) interpretation. The first question you should ask is 'What is the aim of the drawing?' When this has been decided, making the drawing is relatively easy. Cézanne reduced all of nature to a cube, cylinder and cone. Paul Klee 'took his line for a walk'. The pathway will slowly emerge as you examine forms objectively, trying to show the exact relationships between objects, the rhythm of the geometric

LEFT
Rosemary Williams
Aberayron, Wales
Charcoal and gouache on paper, 10×16 inches (25.6×41 cm)
The landscape artist must draw outside in order to respond to the moods and impressions of the landscape. It is not only the atmosphere that is important, but also the power of the light and shade and texture, in revealing the scene. This expressive and dramatic interpretation echoes the violence of the elements, and uses the media with a gestural energy. The inert cottages amalgamate with the hillside, blended together by extremes of climate. The bushes and brambles are petrified and suspended into unnatural configurations through the force of the winds. All are spontaneously captured with vigorous economy in an unusual combination of media.

LEFT
Herbert Folwell
White Mountains, Chania, Crete
Watercolor and pencil, 11½×15½ inches (29.4×39.7cm)
This drawing – or is it a painting? – is an audacious and unusual combination of media and method, using a mixture of aerial and linear perspective. Technically the picture is about contradictions. It is divided in half both through its composition and its contrasting methods of expression, and is a good example of a picture that breaks all the rules. The carefully modeled mountains, painted in delicate watercolor, are the antithesis of the hard-ruled linear lines of the concrete buildings. There is no softening of line or tone or delicate color to ease man's impact on nature. This could be a statement on conservation, although the artist just wanted to capture the beauty of the scene.

structure or the tactile qualities of its texture. Most people have a natural bias toward either an atmospheric interpretation and a love of light and dark or, at its opposite, a feel for pattern and the value of the positive against the negative space.

It is useful to concentrate or focus on the subject from differing positions, trying close up or distant viewpoints and allowing for different emphases on foreground, mid-ground or background. Some subjects demand fine detail, others, broad statements.

Choosing the appropriate medium will also clarify the intention of the drawing, and it is always useful to make several drawings in different media of the same subject so its

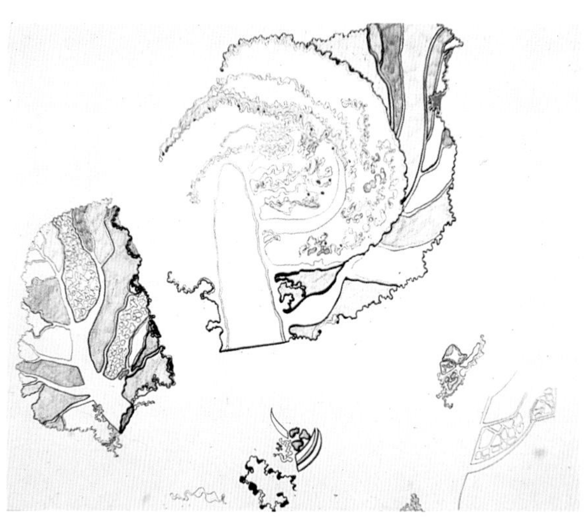

effect and resulting interpretations can be developed. Pencil, inks, charcoal and pastel paints are all exciting to use and can be intermixed and used experimentally in the same way as pigments.

The scale of the drawing is another interesting variation; to work always on the same scale can be predictable and limiting. Extremes of scale can be stimulating, particularly if a close up is made on a large sheet, and a far distant view on a small one.

Drawings can be made for their own sake and can be about many subjects. Hogarth used drawings to make an incisive social commentary on London life. The cartoonist uses the media to exaggerate or lampoon his subject. Another route is to develop the inner thoughts into imaginative works such as those made by William Blake.

One of the main uses of any drawing is as a preparation for further work, either another drawing or, more usually, to lead on into another medium, but skills already discussed and practiced in this chapter are used to gather and develop the necessary information.

FAR LEFT BELOW
Sally Blenkinsop
Kew Gardens
Pencil on paper, 10½×8¼ inches (26.9×21.1cm)
The main aim of this artist is to reveal the rhythm and inner structure of the tree. Each turn of a branch and mass of foliage is thoughtfully analyzed. The negative shapes between the branches and leaves become a potent and powerful element, fundamental to unveiling the underlying geometry and life rhythm unique to this specimen.

CENTER LEFT
Foundation Study: Cross-section of a cabbage
Ink on paper
Cutting through a flower or vegetable presents a way of looking afresh at a familiar subject. This example shows how the inner structure of the cabbage can be expressed as a decorative and rythmic pattern. The student has been encouraged to work decisively because of the permanant character of indian ink.

LEFT
Jill Tweed
Rearing Horse
Watercolor and oil pastel, 27×21 inches (69.1×53.8cm)
This lively impression of a rearing horse exudes movement and tension. The essence of its noble strength and power is captured with bold, direct, energetic marks, set off against the underlying wash of the background and horse. A living subject is enhanced if an impression of movement is created. Observing and recording a subject in motion by noting each change of the body adds significantly to the vitality of the impression. The point of balance just prior to the peak of a movement can be more effective than the most extreme position. Coupled with these observations, the media and the rhythm of marks serve to invigorate the drawing.

5. Perspective

Many people feel intimidated and confused by perspective and the complex diagrams and involved instructions used to teach it. It is important to understand the theories on a basic level, so that they can be used as a broad guide to aid both drawing and painting. Perspective as a systematic, mathematically-based system was invented by the Italian sculptor and architect Filippo Brunelleschi (1377-1446). The earliest painting to apply Brunelleschi's idea of a single vanishing point or central perspective was Masaccio's fresco of *The Trinity* in Sta Maria Novella in Florence, painted in 1527.

Perspective has its own laws, but they are not laws of painting as a whole and many artists will choose not to use them. It is a fact that a cube is a solid contained by six equal sides and all its angles are right angles. Yet when drawn in perspective as if straight on to the viewer, the front edge of the top is bigger than the back edge. The sides are no longer parallel to each other but slope inward and will finally meet at a point called the vanishing point. The front plane of the box remains square with all its sides still equal and opposing ones parallel.

If the same cube is turned at an angle then

BELOW
Kevin Chapman
Last Hours
Watercolor, 12½×15¼ inches (32×39cm)
Here the horizon line of the sea is also the eye level of the painting. All the people on the beach are below this level, their shadows meeting at a single vanishing point. The mood and ambience of the picture is determined by these long shadows created by the low evening light. The color scheme is simple and the background washes are atmospheric, suggesting the onset of dusk.

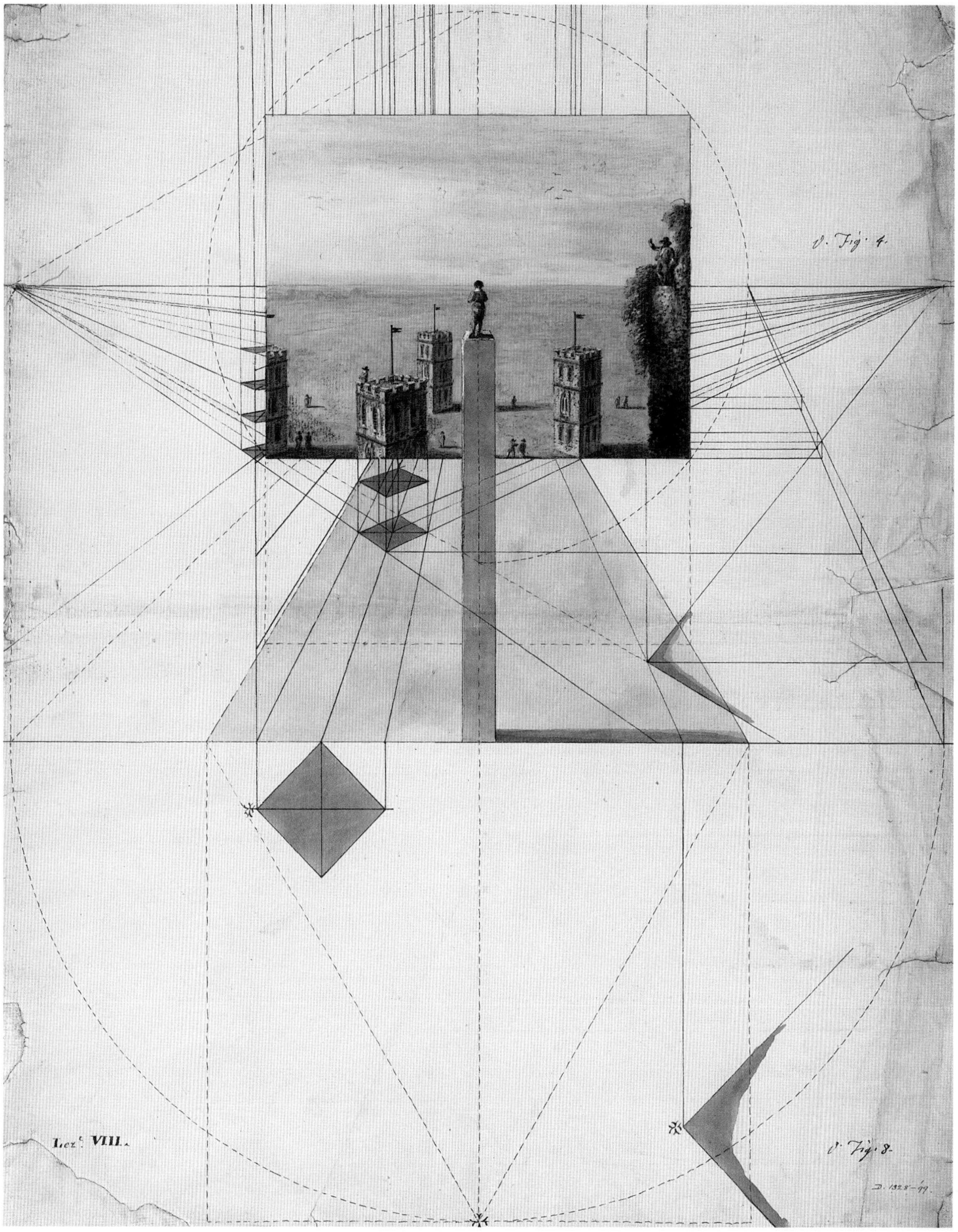

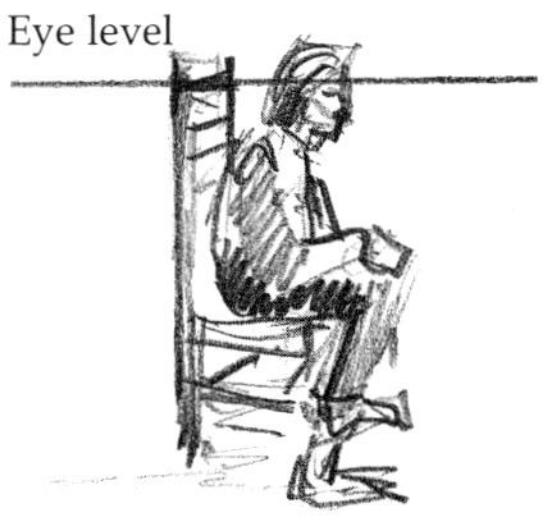

LEFT
Anonymous; Italian
A Lesson in Perspective
Pen and ink and watercolor on laid paper, c. 1780
This fascinating drawing typifies the type of perspective exercise which might have been used in a text book. The drawing shows both linear perspective, and the effect of depth through aerial perspective, by means of graduated bands of color.

only the front edge remains the same length; the sides now also diverge toward the back shorter edge, the diagonals of which will meet at two different vanishing points. Before fully explaining why this happens it is useful to explain the meaning of the terms.

Eye Level

The ground underneath the feet is called the ground plane. If this is completely flat, for example when looking out to sea, the horizon line, where the sea meets the sky, is at the viewer's eye level. This will not vary even if the viewer sits down on the beach, or climbs up the cliffs. Even in a town where the horizon line is hidden by buildings, the eye level will still be in the same position. This can be checked by holding out a pencil horizontally at arm's length.

Vanishing Point

This is the point at eye level where parallel lines will appear to converge as they recede into the distance. Rail tracks or the edges of a straight road will appear to meet at a vanishing point exactly on the horizon or eye level. The laws of perspective developed by Brunelleschi, known as Renaissance or linear perspective, are based on this fixed central viewpoint.

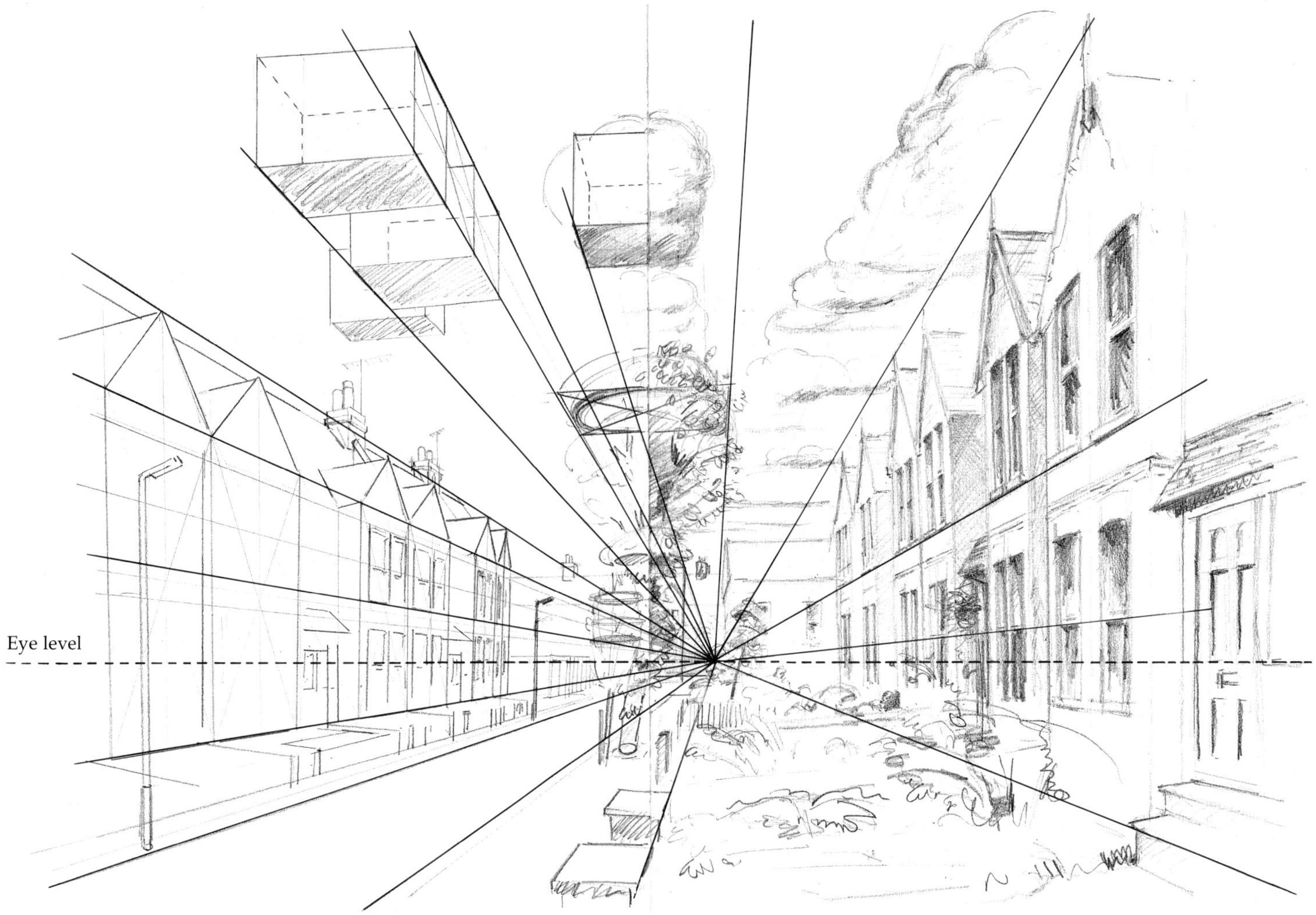

Eye level

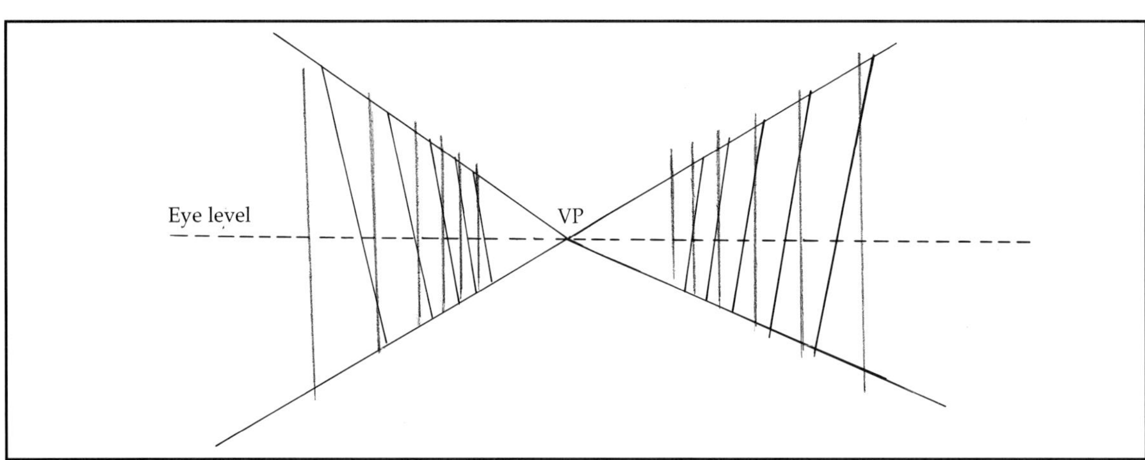

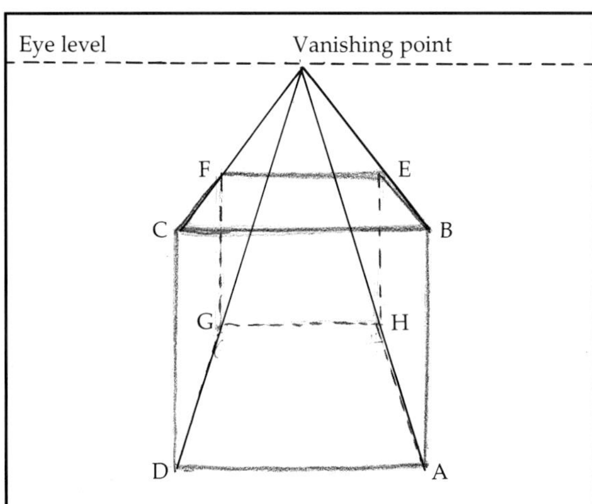

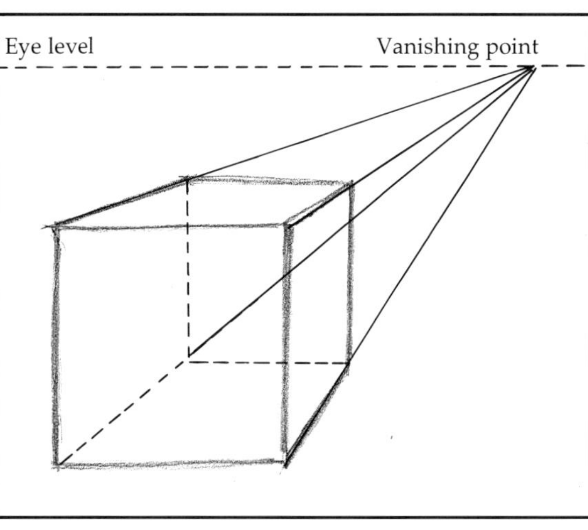

ABOVE

This two-sided drawing of a London street by Elaine Alderson demonstrates the value of understanding and mastering single point perspective and how to apply this knowledge to reality. You must absorb and practice the fundamental basic principles first as illustrated in the diagrams (left). This will enable you to make the drawing of a street by using these principles as an underlying structure for the construction of houses, road, trees and sky. At first your drawing may appear rather wooden or lifeless, but eventually it will come intuitively as you gain confidence and experience. The more experienced artist will be able to make a direct and skilful drawing, as illustrated on the right of this scene. The use of rules of perspective and construction are integrated instinctively into the work. Should part of the subject prove difficult to analyze or draw, the relevant rules may then be used to help solve the problem.

The Picture Plane

This can be likened to an imaginary sheet of glass, positioned squarely at right angles and perpendicular on a chosen spot somewhere between the artist and the subject. The further away it is from the subject then the larger the drawing on it will be. The distance between the two will help to reduce the distortion. As a simple experiment, make a drawing on a window using a soluble overhead projector pen. It is easier to close one eye (monocular vision) to avoid double (binocular) vision. Before drawing the subject, position the eye level at the glass. An object such as a car drawn close to the glass will be bigger in scale than a car further away. A scale change can also be made if you alter position; the closer you are to the glass, the larger the scale of the car will be. When working out the scale of a drawing, both your position and the position of the object must be taken into account in relationship to the picture plane.

Single Point Perspective

A box which is positioned straight on to the view, so that its sides are parallel to each other and to the drawing paper, will have only one point where all the converging lines meet. If a box is positioned below eye level, the top will be seen; if the box is positioned above eye level, the bottom will be seen. Should the box be positioned half above and half below eye level, neither the top nor the bottom will be in view. The closer each box is to the eye level, the less of the top or bottom will be seen; a box with its top at the same level as the eye will appear as a straight line.

Translucent Boxes

Simple geometric forms drawn in perspective can be used as a means of constructing more complex forms when used in conjunction with each other. First it is necessary to be able to draw the inside of the cube as though it is translucent.

First draw a cube as in the diagram (far left). Next join points A and D to the vanishing point. Drop parallel lines from points E and F until they intersect the new diagonals G and H. Finally join G and H, making the inner box complete.

How to Divide Proportionally

One of the most useful exercises to understand is how to divide the box in half so that the front is visually bigger than the back. In reality few artists will put this theory into practice, but through understanding the theory, similar results can be achieved by eye alone. Draw a translucent box. The front plane can be divided into half easily by

BELOW
Tomasso Masaccio
(1401-28?)
Trinity in Santa Maria Novella, Florence, 1428
Fresco

LEFT
Anne Vassallo
The College Corridor
Watercolor, 30×22 inches (76.8×56.3cm)
The simplicity of this subject belies its complex spatial relationships. These have been explored utilizing single-point perspective, tone, and changes in size and scale. For example, the two sets of doors are actually the same size, but give a sense of depth through their change in size. The composition plays on the triangle for its structure, and highlights triangles in the architectural detail and in the shadows thrown across the floor by the doors. The eye is led around and into the picture both by the geometry of its structure, and by the strategically placed accents of dark paint.

measuring it with a ruler. The top poses more of a problem. If it is divided by measuring this would make both sections equal, which means the theory of the front seeming bigger than the back is negated. Division in perspective is made by using the diagonals A to D and B to C. Parallel lines can then be drawn through their intersection, thus dividing the box into four quarters, the front two seeming larger than the back two. The area could be subdivided further by continuing to draw diagonals.

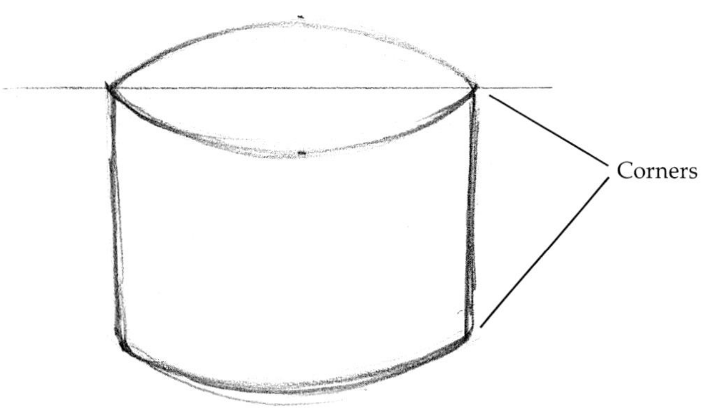

How to put single-point perspective theory into practice

All the examples so far have used the theories of perspective to show how the space is subdivided, but in reality few artists would spend so long in dividing and subdividing. A more realistic approach is to put in the broad lines as observed, then check them by using the pencil held out horizontally or vertically to assess the angles.

The horizontal lines of the top and bottom of windows can be drawn as continuous lines back to the vanishing point. The vertical subdivisions can be put in visually, making sure that as they recede they appear to become smaller and get closer together. This is a much quicker and more lively process than the labored laws of theoretical perspective, but it is valuable to gain some understanding of these via the simple exercises shown.

Interior of a Room A room can be drawn looking straight at the end wall. Objects can be drawn in the room but they must all be positioned square to each other and to the room. The diverging lines must meet exactly at the same vanishing point. The windows and cupboards are subdivided by diagonals to find the proportion of the panes.

Circles and Cylinders in Perspective

First draw a square in perspective and extend it into either a cube or a rectangular box. Lightly draw in the inner construction lines. The top is divided using the diagonals, then intersected by the parallels. The circle is drawn into the square with its edges touching points A B C and D. The front of the circle will appear to be larger than the back section. To extend it into a cylinder the bottom plane needs to be subdivided and the circle drawn. The sides of the cylinder are made by joining A to E and B to F. It is important to note that the top ellipse is shallower than the bottom. A cylinder drawn above eye level will reveal the underside of the ellipses, with those nearer to the eye level being shallower.

The mathematical formula to obtain a perfect square in perspective is complex, so it is worth noting that distortions may occur should the structure be off square.

Drawing Ellipses in Reality

In reality you will draw ellipses free hand and not make complex structures. It is useful, however, to check the freehand drawings for the following points. Firstly, the front half of each ellipse should be visually larger in proportion than the back. This can be done by drawing a faint line horizontally across the center. Secondly, the lowest ellipses should be more rounded than those near to the eye level. Finally, the ellipse should not have corners where it joins the vertical of the cylinder. The ellipse must appear to go behind the vertical and be continuous; a sharp corner visually stops it.

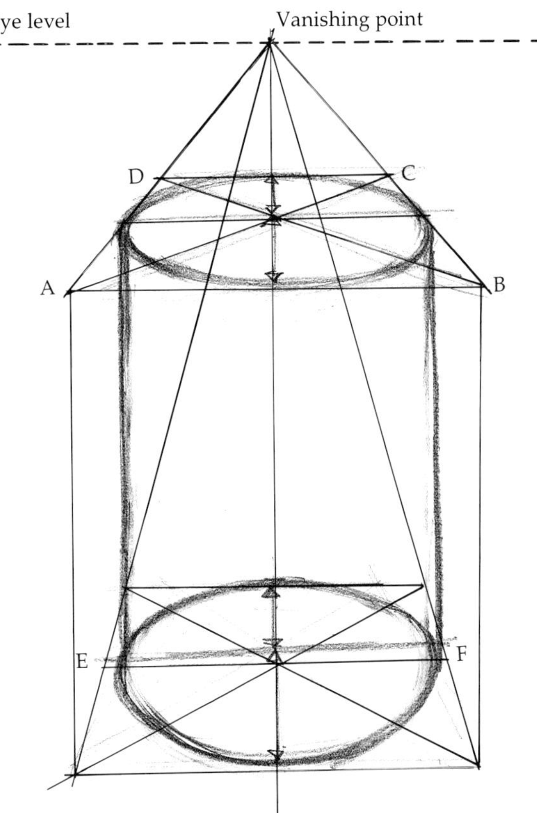

Drawing circles and ellipses
The diagram at left shows how a cylinder is constructed from an extended circle in perspective. It is important to remember that the back half of the ellipse is smaller than the front half, and that ellipses are shallower as they get closer to the eye level. The diagram (below) is a drawing made from reality. The artist has first drawn the simple shapes by eye, then checked them by lightly overlaying the construction lines.

The glass jar clearly shows the differences in the increase of ellipse as they descend in stages below the eye level.

The diagram far left below is an example of how NOT to draw a cylindrical object. It is always better to draw the whole ellipse, even if only part of it is actually seen. This gives a smooth rhythm to the sweep of the circle as it turns away from view.

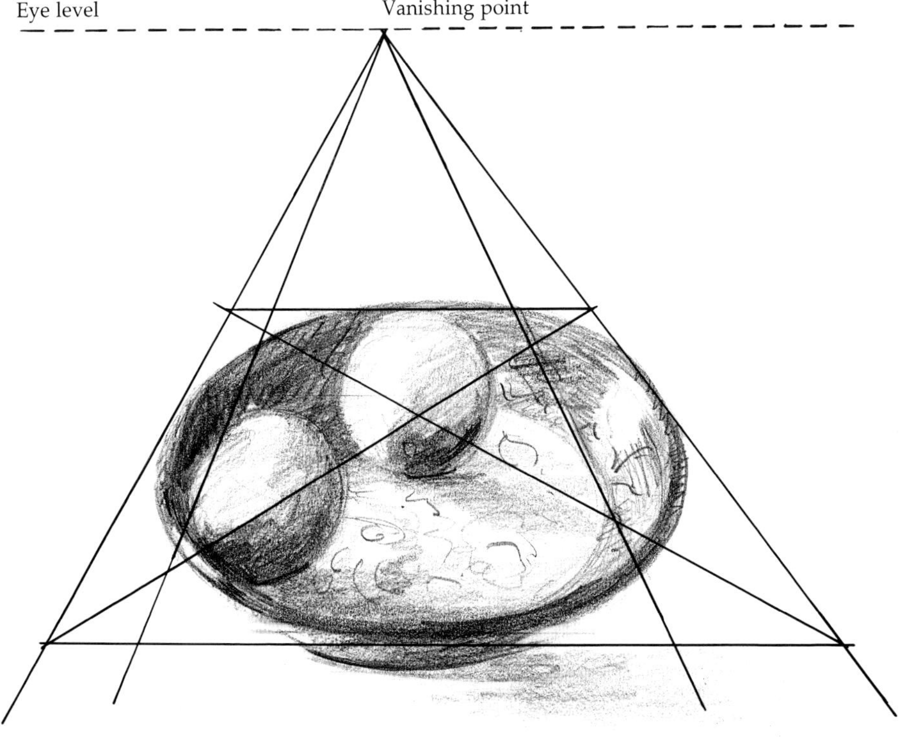

Multipoint Perspective

This allows for objects to be drawn at angles to the viewer and more complex arrangements can be analyzed. When a cube is drawn at an angle, two sides will be visible but only the verticals will be parallel to each other and the paper. All other lines will diverge to vanishing points at the eye level. Each side will have its own vanishing points, with the invisible structure lines also meeting at them. Objects or boxes at differing angles will each have their own vanishing points, so a drawing of a room with a jumble of furniture will have many vanishing points along the horizon line. The closer together the vanishing points are, the more acute and distorted the angles of the objects will become. Vanishing points in a real situation can be widely spaced and are frequently located well off the paper.

When three planes of the cube are still visible, there are three sets of converging lines, meaning that none of the lines are parallel to each other. This is used when a tall building is viewed above or below.

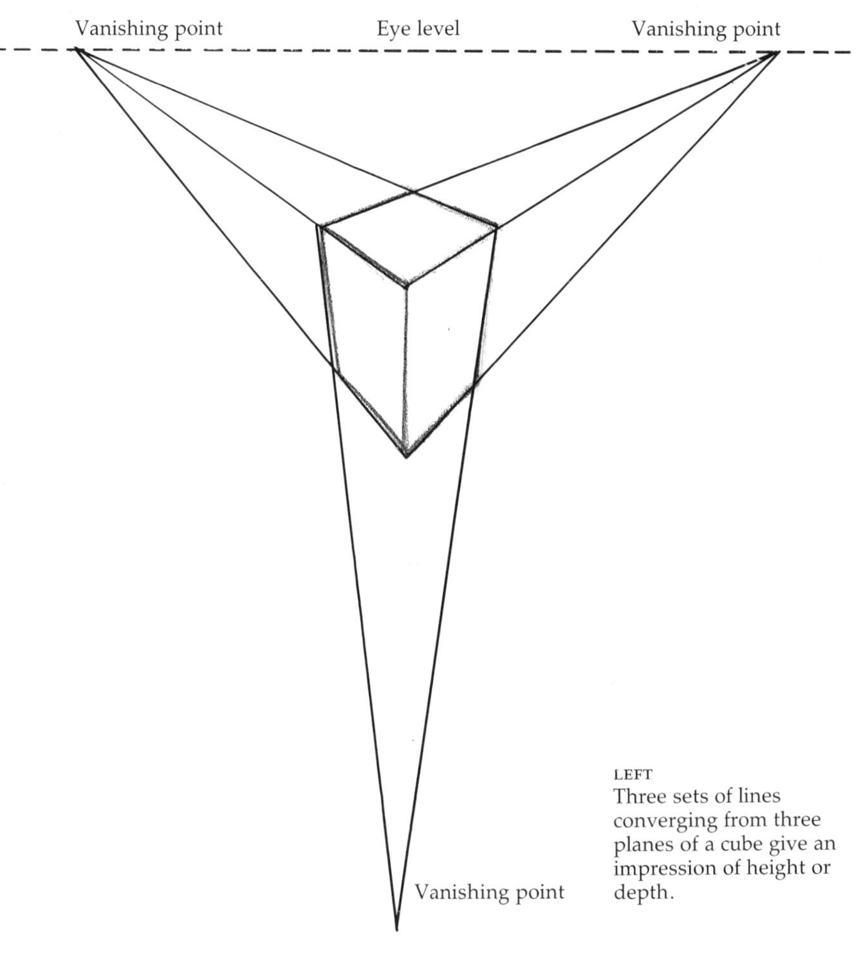

LEFT
Three sets of lines converging from three planes of a cube give an impression of height or depth.

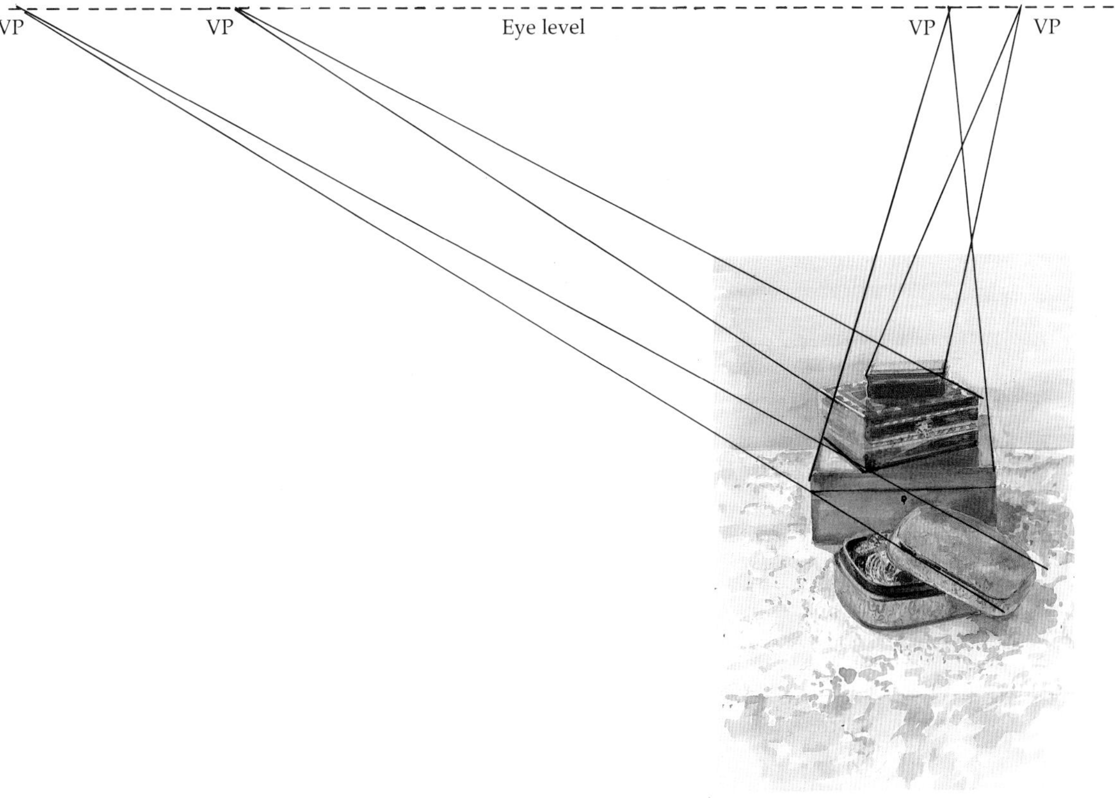

FAR LEFT
Kevin Chapman
Kew
Watercolor and gouache, 9½×13 inches (24.3×33.3cm)
Buildings in a landscape enhance their setting. The structure and perspective of the former gives a sense of scale to the latter. The strong and simple foreground, together with its bold tonal changes, focuses on the subject without adding to its complexity. Although the painting is unfinished in places, there is enough underpainting and structure to complete the composition. The moody result evokes the past architectural glory of the building as it is set among the rustling trees of today. Techically the artist has combined a range of washes, scumbling salt, sgraffito in both translucent and opaque watercolors.

ABOVE LEFT
Elaine Alderson
Still Life with Boxes
Watercolor
This is a simple exercise for the beginner to put the theory of perspective into practice. First draw in lightly the simple shapes to determine their proportions and vanishing points. Tones and detail can then be laid in directly with paint.

LEFT
Maurits Escher
Cubic Space Division
Lithograph, 10¼×10¼ (26.6×26.6cm)
This deceptively simple composition is obsessively subtle in its use of perspective and tone. Repetitive cubes are locked meticulously into a grid that defines the space precisely. The careful use of multi-point perspective gives great depth both through and down into the structure. The third vanishing point is located far below the subject, resulting in a gradual convergence of the verticals.

Tonally, the picture is remarkable. The surface of each cube is a slightly different tone and each interlinking support graduates evenly from dark through to light. As a result, the viewer seems to be suspended eternally in space.

Construction of a House and Pitched Roof

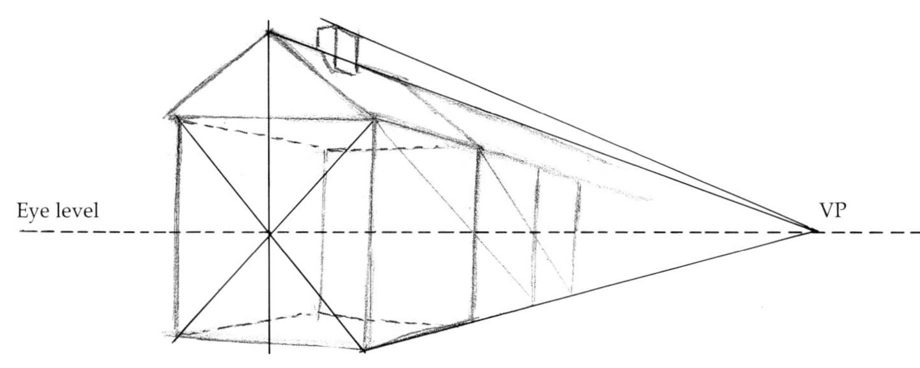

A simple theoretical house can be constructed using single-point perspective and division by diagonals.

Draw a box at eye level and lightly draw in the invisible perspective lines. Divide the front and back planes in the diagram (see right) by measuring and extend the center

LEFT
Joan Milroy
Washing
Watercolor, 25×18 inches (64×46.1cm)
Multipoint perspective has been used for this picture. Artists frequently use two or three vanishing points for tall (or very low) subject matter. When you are standing close to a high building the vertical lines no longer seem parallel, but converge toward a point high in the sky. Should the same building be viewed from the top looking down, then the vertical lines would converge toward a point below the ground.

The sense of space here is further enhanced by graduating the tones from dark to light in both the sky and the buildings. These come together in the top right hand corner, creating a focal point of the fresh luminosity of the washing.

RIGHT
Rosemary Williams
The Borders
Watercolor, 3×6 inches (7.7×15.4cm)
This small sketchbook study is an example of aerial or atmospheric perspective. The space in the subject is exaggerated by the juxtaposition of cool blues in the background set against the deliberately heightened warm colors in the foreground.

line up higher than the top edge of the box on both the front and back planes. Join the top of each I/S together and to the vanishing points. The pitch of the roof is informed by lines joined from I to both C and B for the front and from J to H and G for the back. A chimney stack can be treated as another box balanced on the pitch. Make sure all diagonals meet at the vanishing point.

A second house can be drawn with the roof on the side. The only difference in constructing the house is in the division of the side of the box. Because it is at an angle, it must be divided by using the diagonals to determine the visual halves of the plane.

Vanishing point

Vanishing point

LEFT
Elaine Alderson
Study of a Chair
Watercolor
Mastery of the simple box diagram with two vanishing points is the structural foundation of this more complex object. It is easy for the beginner to draw its legs, arms, back or front in isolation from each other. Indicating a basic box understructure helps to relate the subject, and its parts, to the overall direction of each plane, and encourages the artist to consider each pair of arms or legs and to draw them in relationship to each other.

Aerial Perspective

This was probably discovered by the Flemish painters of the fifteenth century and then developed by Leonardo da Vinci in his landscapes. The method consists of paling and blurring the definition of receding objects so that they look as though they are veiled in an atmosphere. The further away they are, the fewer the tonal contrasts used. The colors used will be selected from a cooler blue palette. Objects in the foreground will retain their full color and definition and colors will range from browns through to greens and on to the distant blues.

Objects in the foreground could be developed and painted with a richer texture. Larger paint or pencil marks which diminish in scale on distant objects also help to create an illusion of depth and space.

6. Color

Color is the most exciting development of the twentieth century in painting, film and television, with new and exciting additions regularly being developed and manufactured. These now seem to supersede the painterly principles of color theory, the luminous metallic paints, heat sensitive dyes and fluorescent colors being difficult to categorize. They should all be experimented with by an artist, and coupled to the theory, rather than subjected to it. Adding a new pigment to a familiar mix can offer new pathways for exploration.

When starting to paint in full color the artist is confronted with two major problems: firstly learning to develop an understanding of the behavior of colors; and, secondly, relating the bright colors of the palette to the real world, which by contrast seems full of subtle neutral shades.

Several influential artists have formalized and developed color both theoretically and practically. These include Michel Eugène Chevreuil (1786-1889), the Impressionists and in particular Georges Seurat (1859-1891) and Claude Monet (1840-1926), and the Bauhaus teachers Paul Klee (1879-1940) and Josef Albers (1888-1976). The theory and technique are best followed through simple practical examples, but all can be developed in great depth. Color is a complex, vital and rich subject for exploration through its various theories in the same way as the development of perspective and depth. Color

Antonia Black
Konya Kleim
Watercolor, 22×30 inches (56.3×76.8cm)
Pattern and color are powerful partners, controled in this picture through the structure created by the horizontal bounds of the composition and the intensity of the white jug. Although central to the painting, the artist has bravely left this unpainted. This gives the eye a rest from the energetic background and allows the remaining scatter of white to become a positive force within the picture.

also makes an important contribution to the creation of a three-dimensional sense of space on a flat surface.

The number and quality of colors are continually being developed and refined. Historically artists could only use the limited palettes available to them. Until around 1200 AD the number of colors was limited to the earth colors and blue frit and white lead, both manufactured by the Egyptians. White lead was the most important single pigment ever discovered because of its opacity and covering power. Prior to its discovery, white was made from chalk. White lead was the only white in easel painting until the discovery of zinc white in 1830 and titanium white in 1916. Between 1200 and 1350 the chromatic range expanded and the palette then remained stable until 1704 when Prussian blue was discovered, replacing the expensive azurite and real ultramarine; a synthetic method was not found for the latter until 1828.

Looking at paintings in the light of the discovery of new pigments adds an interesting new dimension to their meaning. Turner, for example, made full and exciting use of the new yellows being developed in the early nineteenth century. The only major development of a new material since then to challenge the creative and technical powers of the artist has been the development of acrylic paints in this century and their popularity and accessibility since the mid 1950s.

Manufacturers produce ranges of paints to suit all markets. The price of a paint usually reflects both its quality and the richness of its pigment. Cheaper paints usually contain more binder than pigment, which affects both covering power and intensity.

Paints may be classed as either artist's color, which is expensive, or student's color, which is cheaper. Some watercolors are fugitive – they will fade if exposed to sunlight and are classed accordingly.

Class AA – Very permanent (24 colors)
Class A – Permanent (47 colors)
Class B – Moderately permanent (10 colors)
Class C – Fugitive (6 colors)

Choosing the First Palette

The first decision should be which water-based paints to choose (see Materials and Equipment, page 16). Many beginners enjoy exploring several categories before making a final choice. Waterbased media are interchangeable and can be used together in a multi-media painting.

J M W Turner (1775-1851)
Falls of the Anio
Watercolor
Turner's watercolors paralleled his painting in oils in their freedom and subtlety of color and expression and their extraordinary imaginative power.

The final decision as to which medium to choose can only really be made by handling the paint. This can be achieved through a simple experimental painting made in each medium, concentrating only on the tonal values of the subject. One white and one color is needed – perhaps a cobalt blue or alizarin. A simple subject should be chosen, such as a couple of boxes and some fruit. These can be painted in each medium, exploring some of the basic techniques, such as washes and brushwork to suggest texture and volume. There is the added value that this exercise continues to develop fundamental skills such as observing the relationships of objects, their proportion, texture, tone and perspective, brought together in a strong composition. The jug and tankard on page 51 provide an example.

Choosing Basic Colors

The large range of colors is bemusing for the beginner. Probably no more than ten or eleven colors are really necessary, plus black and white. Some of the most exciting paintings have been made from five or less. Good examples were painted by Thomas Girtin (1775-1802), who worked with just five colors. He achieved richness and variation by superimposing washes as transparent colors to create subtle mixtures. There is no one answer as to exactly which colors you should buy; your preferences will be based on two factors, the subject matter to be painted and the characteristics and nature of the paint. It is better to buy two or three colors first and learn how to use and develop their potential before adding more to the range.

There is, however, a logic to mixing and using color which can begin to be explained with some basic theoretical exercises. These are useful to practice and the results can be kept in the paint box for future reference.

BELOW
Maggie Scott
The Red Boat
Watercolor, 30×22 inches (76.8×56.3cm)
This large confident painting is based on a simple subject and a limited palette, consisting of the three primary colors, red, blue and yellow, plus viridian green. The waves of subtle color are either dilute washes of these four or intermixes of them. Opposite colors on a color circle are called complementaries; when mixed they seem to neutralize each other, resulting in the soft broken colors used in the waves.

Through first making, and then using with understanding, a simple color wheel it is possible to work out color relationships and be able to mix the subtle colors of nature. These, surprisingly, are mixed from the bright primaries and secondaries, and not by adding black, which simply makes colors darker.

When discussing color the following terms are used:

HUE This term distinguishes one color from another.

CHROMA Refers to the intensity of the HUE; red has an intense chroma, gray none at all.

TONE Refers to the light and dark half-tones, called values.

ACHROMATIC SCALE Refers to black and white, and the scale of grays in between the two. Neither contain any trace of pigment.

Theoretically, all colors can be made from the three main colors. In reality this is difficult, but the basic principles are easier to understand when based on the three. They are known as the primaries, and can be defined as follows.

Primary Colors

These are the colors which cannot be made by mixing other colors (see Color Mixing, page 55). There are two sets of primaries. One relates to pigments; these are red, blue and yellow, and when they are mixed together they will make black. The second set of primaries refers to lights and consists of red, blue and green; when these are all mixed they make white (light).

Deciding which of the manufacturers' pigments are the primaries is more of a problem, due to the wide selection they offer. Some of the range are light, others are dark (tone), others appear to be less intense (chroma). Those remaining will be intense and will need careful selection to decide which is the purest color; for example, yellow is the midway point between red and blue and should have no hint of either in its mix. When you have chosen your primary red, blue and yellow, paint each of them into one third of a circle in a flat intense wash and note the name of the paint (a notebook is invaluable for all experiments). The following colors are worth considering for the first palette, plus white:

Cadmium Yellow
Cadmium Red
Cobalt Blue

But color will vary according to manufacturer, so look carefully at the pigments to try and decide if they are the purest form of each yellow, red and blue.

Further colors are made by intermixing the primaries, and are known as secondary colors.

Secondary Colors

These are colors made by mixing two primary colors in equal amounts. Paint this mix into the center position of a ring surrounding the primaries. The resulting mix will be orange, green and a brownish purple. The mixing can be continued by adding primaries in proportionate amounts to the secondary. The results, using orange as an example, would make the orange more yellow-orange, as more yellow was mixed, or more red-orange, as more red was mixed.

When secondary colors are mixed, a third range of colors are made, called tertiary or broken colors.

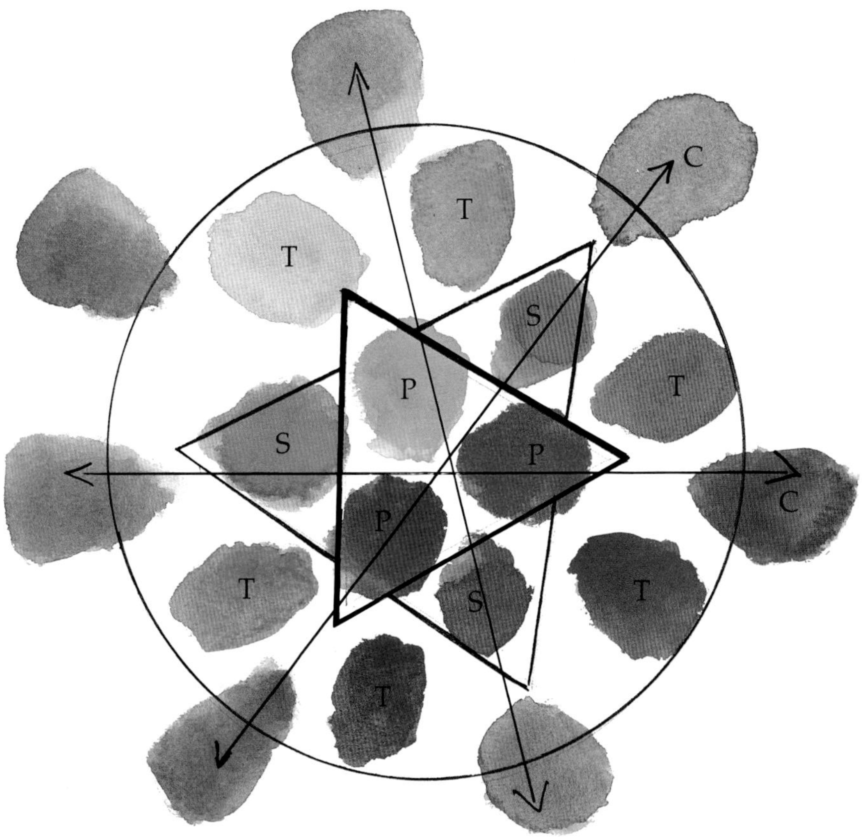

Tertiary or Broken Color

These are the colors that most closely match the subtle shades found everywhere in the natural world. They are made by mixing the secondary colors together. The resulting mixes tend toward a neutral or gray color; their chroma is low, they are colors that have lost their brightness. If a little white gouache is added to the mix, they will look close to a gray. Broken color is the technique of dragging one color across another. The two can then be mixed optically by the viewer to make a third color. Georges Seurat and his fellow Impressionists developed optical mixing in depth. Small dots of color were painted next to each other so that the eye and brain could not identify then individually and a new color combination materialized. The resulting paintings were rich and vibrant with rich atmospheric effect.

ABOVE
This basic color wheel shows the primary, secondary, tertiary and complementary colors. These last are mixtures of opposites within the wheel – reds with greens, blues with oranges and yellows with purples. They neutralize each other to create soft grays and the subtle shades we see all around us.

LEFT
New media: experiment with one color plus white when trying a new medium. This tonal painting is based on exploring overlying washes to create depth of tone. Only one blue has been used. You can then add a few more colors to your palette, including reds and greens and possibly another blue.

The Intermediate Palette

As mentioned before, the three primary colors have practical limitations, but it is useful to work and gain experience with them through a number of exercises and paintings. The color wheel (illustrated on page 51) is valuable but the following ideas might also be developed.

1 Collect a group of simple objects in orange, green and purple. Arrange them and make a painting using the basic palette of three primaries.

2 Collect another group of objects which are ranges of gray or neutral color and make a second picture.

3 Mix up all the objects from the two previous exercises to form a final group, and make another picture.

Hot and Cold Colors

It soon becomes evident that although secondary and tertiary colors can be mixed, the range being used has limitations. For example a lemon is a very different kind of yellow from the primary chrome yellow. A cardboard box or wooden crate is yet another and different yellow. These colors can be described as a cold yellow for the lemon and a warm yellow for the box. All colors have these properties of heat or cold. Looking at the color wheel, all the colors nearest the reds are hotter than those in the area of the blues. It is not possible to say all blues are cold, because those nearer to the red will be warmer than those nearest to the yellow.

When buying more color to extend your range it is useful to buy only more reds, blues and yellows. All the seductive purples, pinks, greens and earth colors can be bought later. Remember, it is easier to understand color mixing step by step. Learn how to use a few, and master them by understanding their properties and characteristics.

BELOW
David Wise
Still Life with Blue Jug
Watercolor, 30×22 inches (76.8×56.3cm)
Comparing this painting with *Irises* (far right), by the same artist and based on similar subject matter, size and techniques, demonstrates clearly that opposite moods can be created through overall color schemes. *Still Life with Blue Jug* is composed from a cool harmonious palette of blues and greens, whilst *Irises* consists mostly of hot vibrant yellows and oranges. Each painting has touches of its complementary colors, either reds or violets, carefully introduced and used to enhance and gently invigorate the work.

White gouache

The following are a suggestion as to choosing six more colors based on their properties of hot and cold.

Hot	Primary	Cold
Yellow orcher	Cadmium yellow	Lemon yellow
Vermilion red	Cadmium red	Alizarin crimson
Ultramarine blue	Cobalt blue	Cerulean blue

Make more paintings with subject matter composed of ranges of primaries, secondaries and tertiaries. Really get to know what happens if yellow ocher is mixed with the reds and blues.

A simple grid mix exercise is easy to paint. Put masking tapes vertically on to a paper at equal distances, and paint a range of reds, blues and yellows into each space. Take off the tapes when the paint is dry and paint stripes across horizontally in the same range of colors. The results give a range of intermixes and show how the same color across itself is intensified. All sorts of combinations can be tried in such a grid mix and black and white can also be included.

Hot and cold colors will also give a sense of space to the picture; the hot colors will come forward in a picture, while the cool colors recede. Long before theories were evolved to deal with color scientifically, the Venetian painters of the Renaissance were using warm and cool paint in opposition to create a sense of form and space. This was fully developed in the nineteenth century by the Impressionists and Post Impressionists, who used color for its own sake and not in a literal descriptive or emotive way. They also used heightened colors, the primaries and secondaries, to paint their environment. Many examples show the power of hot and cold to define the volume, space or mood of the subject. Really getting to know the nine colors selected, plus white, will give a firm foundation for future work; many other colors can be added as needed.

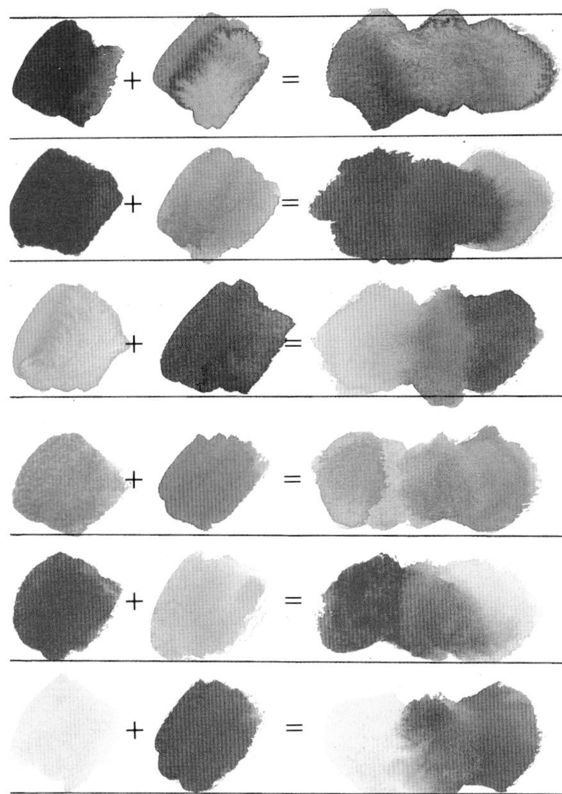

LEFT
Color chart
This exercise is a quick method of familiarizing yourself with new colors, and examining their properties when intermixed by letting two washes run into each other.

BELOW
David Wise
Irises
Watercolor, 30×22 inches (76.8×56.3cm)

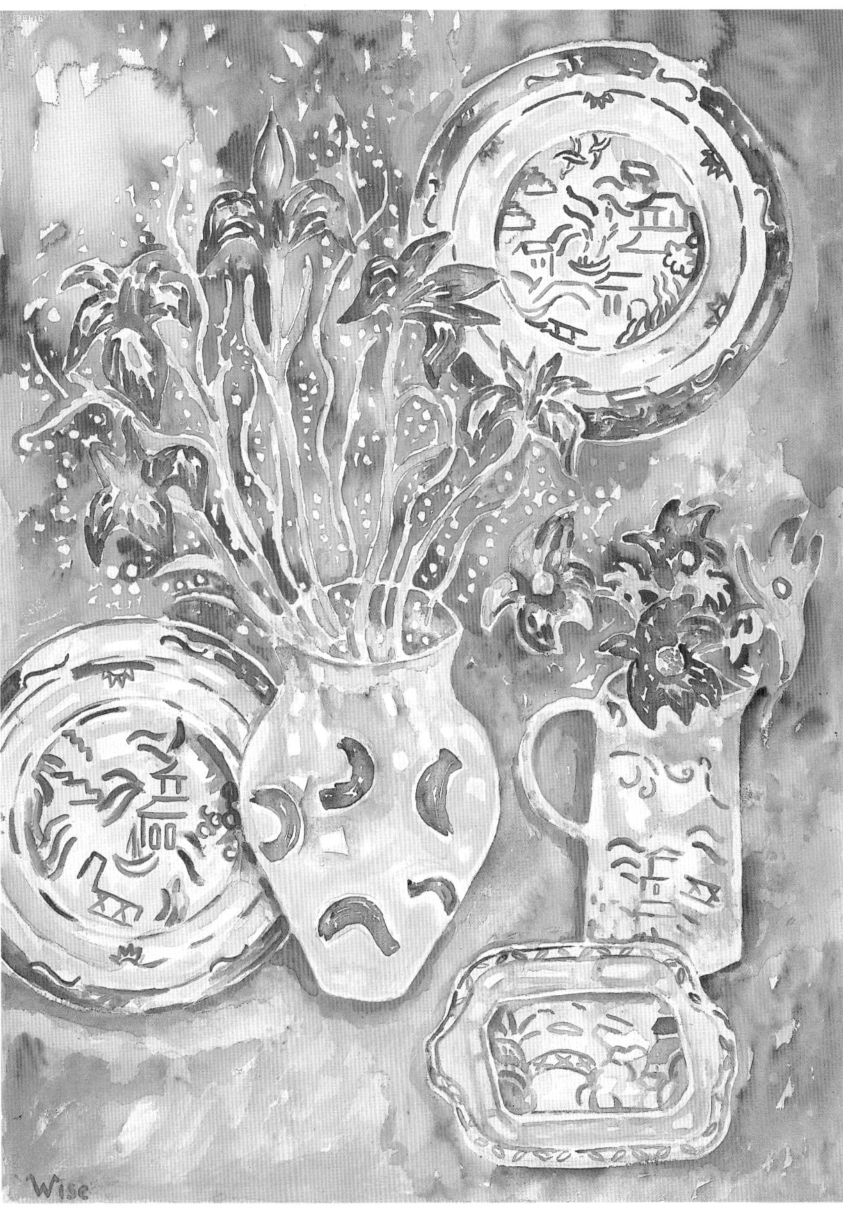

The Advanced Palette

Further reds, blues and yellows may be added, but it is also useful at this stage to buy some of the earth colors, raw or burnt sienna and raw or burnt umber: four lovely rich traditional colors, ideal for landscape work, as is Payne's gray. There are also a few colors that seem impossible to mix, such as fuchsia, magenta and some purples. If the subject matter demands, then it probably is worth buying one from this range.

So far there has been no mention of buying greens. This is a color of nature, which is why it has not been included. The greens of the pigments are usually much brighter than the subtler greens of the landscape. The beginner finds it only too easy to dip a brush into a color and put it straight on to the painting and the results will look brash and unnatural if the green has not been mixed before use. With several blues and yellows on the palette you are more likely to think the mix through first; for example, if the green is toward blue or toward yellow, which yellow should be added to which blue. The resulting painting will certainly be richer. Colors can also be toned down, not by the addition of black but by adding a spot of their opposite color on the color wheel, known as their complementaries. There is one green that cannot be easily mixed and that is viridian green.

The advanced palette may therefore consist of a selection from the colors mentioned above, but it is always worth adding more should the subject demand it, for example Venetian red, Prussian or monastral blue.

Black

Black is a wonderful color in its own right, but when mixed with other colors it makes them darker and can make them appear dingy; a little black goes a long way. Black can be made by mixing the three primaries. The result will be either bluish black, reddish black or yellow-brown black and thus more natural for use in an environmental context.

White

White mixed into colors will make them lighter, but will not change them in any other way. Because it is opaque, however, it can help to 'reveal' colors when a little is mixed into tertiary or complementary grays.

Black and White: Achromatic Scale

Black added to white makes gray, and a scale of grays can be made by adding measured amounts of black to white. All colors will re-

BELOW
Experiment with ranges of blues mixed with yellows and then 'neutralized' with minute touches of complementary reds. This can be coupled with exploring various types of plant and foliage and practicing brush control.

RIGHT
For this grid color mixing exercise, use tapes to divide the space, then paint the same colors across and down.

RIGHT BELOW
Francis Bowyer
Beachcombing
Watercolor, 12½×9 inches (32×23cm)
This color scheme is economic and purposeful, evoking a warm summer day through using warm ultramarine blue and yellow ocher. These two main colors are 'activated' by bold selective dashes of vermilion red in the focal points of the composition.

late tonally to one of the grays on the achromatic scale. Half close your eyes when assessing the color against the gray and the two should look tonally equal. This is valuable while working on a painting when colors need adjusting one against another; for example yellow relates to a lighter tone of gray than its complementary violet. If white is added to the latter is will 'hold its place' in the picture field by its interaction with the yellow, whereas if left darker it would merely recede.

Organization of the Palette

Developing good working procedures, such as cleaning brushes and paintboxes and stretching paper, also includes organizing colors on the palette. There are no set rules and you will find your own sequence, but the important point is that this happens. Watercolor boxes containing pans of color can be organized so the paints are logically arranged. If gouache, acrylic or tubes of watercolors are used, then varying amounts of color need squeezing on to a plate, palette or suitable surface. Most artists like to work from their lightest colors to the darkest; from white through yellows, reds, blues, greens and earth colors to black. Each painting will have dominant colors, so vary the amounts on the palette accordingly.

Mixing Colors

The colors that we see around us are not found in tubes or pans of paint. To mix them you need to start with the heightened color nearest to the subject, and decide whether it is hot or cold. A dash of its complementary will neutralize the color a little or a lot, thus making it seem more natural.

Once the full range of colors has been assembled, very accurate color mixing can be explored. It is best to concentrate totally on mixing the color and forget the problems of shape, proportion, perspective and composition. A plant or object can be analyzed, with each color recorded as a spot or splodge of color which can be put down in a random or organized way on the paper. Thus all your energy and concentration is focused on careful color matching. Narrow strips of white paper are useful, so that as colors are mixed they can be laid along the edge of the paper and held close against the subject for comparison. Watercolor will be a tone lighter when it dries and this needs to be taken into account. Accurate color mixing will build your speed and confidence.

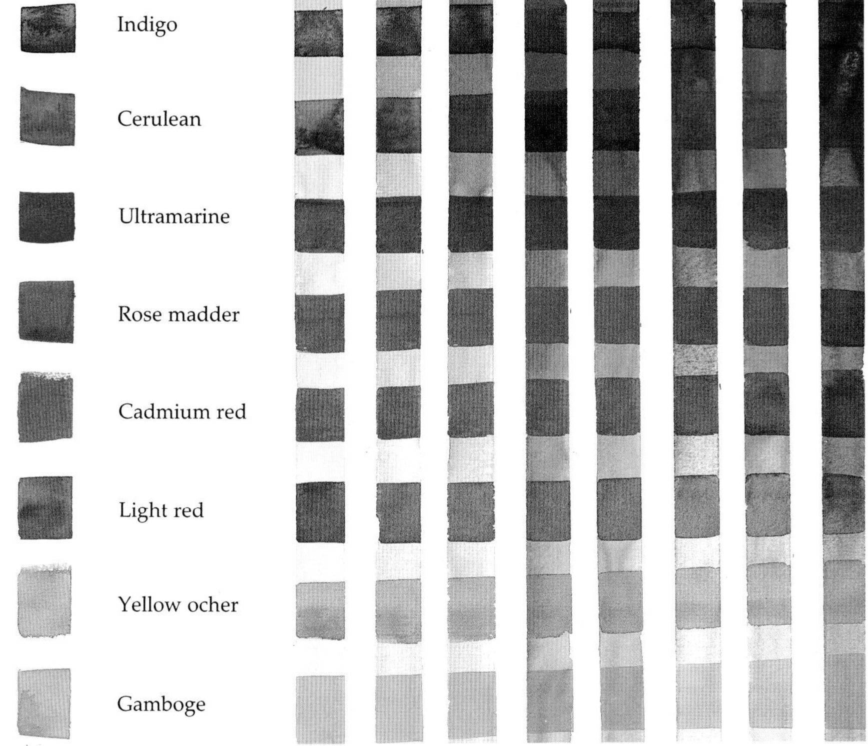

Overlays of transparent washes will also create new mixes of color, and again it is helpful to analyze an object by concentrating on the colors and putting them down in a random or structured way, divorced from the shape of the actual object.

Harmonious Color

Color harmony is created by groups of color adjacent to each other on the color wheel; these colors will co-exist together comfortably. Examples include reds through to oranges, yellows through to greens, blues through to purples. When used as the focus of a painting, they create a sense of atmosphere and unity. Ranges of harmonious colors are also used to great effect by designers, both architectural and theatrical, to give a large number of elements a feel of unity.

Complementary Colors

Each primary color has a complementary, the one directly opposite to it on the color wheel. Examples include red and green, blue and orange, and yellow and violet. When each pair is mixed together they will neutralize each other and the resulting color will be close to a gray. To see the color fully a little opaque white could be added. The mix has a low chroma. It is useful to use these terms when solving the mixing problems associated with the subtle colors of objects in nature. A neutral colored fence, weathered and silvery, may start being mixed from a warm blue, ultramarine, with its cool complementary, a yellow orange, to neutralize it, plus white.

Simultaneous Contrast: Complementary Color

If pairs of complementary colors are painted next to each other with their edges touching, a totally different phenomenon occurs, giving a dazzling energy force across the picture. This is known as simultaneous contrast. Constable, for example, is renowned for using a little red in his green landscapes, so the picture is subtly enlivened.

After-image

Another interesting attribute relating to complementary color happens more slowly. If you look at one color, red for example, intently for 30 seconds or more and then transfer your gaze to a neutral surface such as white or gray, its complementary color, green, will be clearly seen. This is due to the structure of the eye. The cones, its color receptors, are tuned to receive either reds, greens or blue-violets. When staring at red the red sensitive cones tire, so with the sudden shift of vision from red to neutral the eye 'sees' only the mixture of green-blue.

A new color is created when the after-image is imposed on a hue; for example if a blue after-image is transferred to a yellow field, it will seem to look green.

Colors with an intense chroma will have a strong effect on more neutral color with a low chroma. If gray is surrounded with orange it appears tinged with the color. If the same gray is surrounded by green, it will look more green. Although the grays are in fact the same, they will appear to vary in their tone because of the different surroundings. If two greens are put close together they will blend together, whereas if green is put next to magenta the color will intensify, so the same green will look as if it is quite a different color depending on its surrounding color.

Brian Fielding
Gray Stripes
Acrylic on canvas, 26×18 inches (66.6×46.1cm)
Each gray stripe is made from mixtures of all the different pairs of complementary colors. White has then been added to them, serving the dual purpose of helping to 'reveal' the gray while the complementaries are being intermixed, and controling the tonal balance of one stripe to the next within the context of the painting. The hard edges of each stripe were achieved by using masking tape. Acrylic dries quickly and is tough, so tapes can be repositioned fairly quickly.

Subtractive and Additive Mixing

Mixing pigments is known as subtractive mixing; they will get darker when more color is added. Mixing all three primaries results in black. Optical mixing of light done by eye is called additive mixing and works in the opposite way; the lights in all colors mixed together will result in white. The effects of optical mixing of color by eye follow neither pigment nor light theory precisely due to the biological structure of the light and color receptors, reds being receptive to light and dark and cones to one of each color. This explains why, if you half close your eyes, the color values of the subject will diminish so its tone can be analyzed.

Shadows

Shadows are created by the light falling on the opposite side of the subject. They help to show the volume of the subject, give weight to the form, and help to define the space and perspective of the surface or plane adjacent to the subject. They can feature as an integral element of the composition and always add to the dimension of the space.

Shadows can be painted in a darker tone of the local or inherent color of the subject; for example, a tomato is red, so the darker side could be made by adding either black or the complementary color, green to darken the area. Another method is to change the color temperature so as the form turns away the color becomes colder; the red tomato could then have a blue, red or purple shadow.

A bolder solution is to paint the shadow in the complementary color, in this example, green. Because the tomato is a hot red, the green will be a blue green such as viridian. The Impressionists experimented in endless ways to find colors to convey dark and light, hot and cold. Wonderful examples can be found in Monet's work, such as the *Haystack* series, where colors were interposed as the light and atmospheric conditions constantly changed.

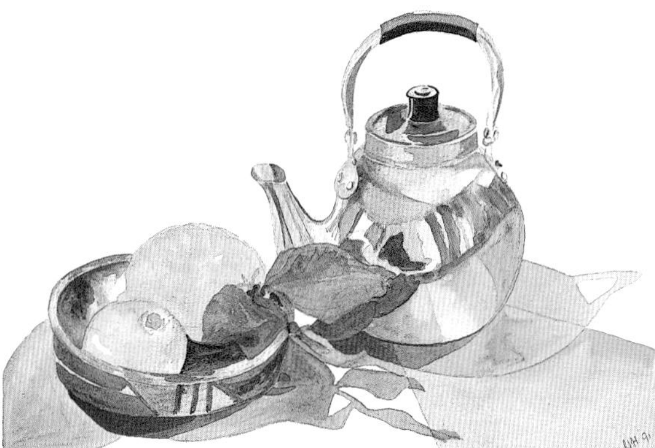

ABOVE
Kevin Chapman
The Tank
Watercolor and gouache, 13×20 inches (33.3×51.2cm)
This is a spirited composition of opposites. The bold vibrant relationships of complementaries red/green and blue/orange create a visual energy and pull the eye around and right into the picture. The furthest hills are painted red, not blue, as would be expected, and their line acts as a counterbalance to the powerful diagonal shadows. The calm center of the composition is a simple fluid flat wash of green that seems to pour down into the tank. The result is dynamic and unsettling, the landscape seeming to hover between reality and illusion.

LEFT
Rita Hodson
Copper Kettle
Watercolor, 13×19 inches (33.3×48.6cm)
Lively shadows can be created using one complementary against another. The shadows in this painting solve the central area of the composition by enhancing both the subject and a love of pattern.

7. Composition

The aim of a good composition is threefold. Firstly, it should capture the essence of the subject's attraction for the artist. Secondly, it should present the subject in a visually interesting arrangement. Thirdly, it should develop the relations of the objects both to each other and to the background or negative space so that the final picture conveys the artist's interpretation of the subject.

There are no set rules about what makes a good composition. Many theories and systems have been developed historically, but in practical terms you need to evolve your own personal priorities and ideas. You should take account of intensity of color, tone, geometry, strength of line, quality of brush strokes, texture, space and narrative detail: a broad range of variables resulting in complex choices and results. The fixed element is the size and shape of the paper or the subject in different positions and from a variety of viewpoints. As a matter of course you should always look at the subject from all points of the compass to find the most interesting or random composition. Objects can be repositioned and quick sketches made recording the new relationships. Frequently the first arrangements will look static and contrived, but developing ideas through a change of viewpoint or regrouping is refreshing. Preliminary sketches should be proportional in scale to the subject and take no longer than 10 or 15 minutes each. The position of the focal point of interest needs careful consideration and large darks and lights or broad color patterns indicated.

Thumbnail sketches can be made by using either a small card with a proportional window or the hands positioned to create a rectangular hole (see diagrams right). Even quick sketches can offer a limited opportunity for analysis of the subject.

Historical Theories

Mathematics has played a role in the historical evolution of theories and formulae governing composition. The quest for perfect harmony was fully developed by the Greeks and its mathematical formulae attributed to Euclid. In simple terms the proportions of the subject are obtained by geometry; the resulting rectangle contains a square and another rectangle which is in the same proportion as the large rectangle. This is known as the golden section. In layman's

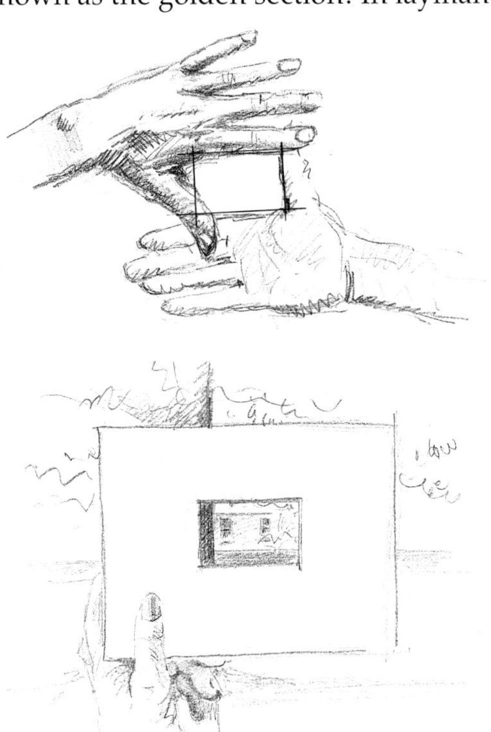

The hands held together, as illustrated left above, can create a useful frame to mask a view or subject. A cardboard mask (left below) does the same job and should be kept with your drawing/painting materials. The series of sketches (bottom) show a simple still life as seen from various viewpoints.

RIGHT BELOW
This sketchbook drawing was made on location and gives succinct information on composition, tone, texture and color which will be developed further in the studio. It also adheres perfectly to the geometric rules for harmonious proportion. Square ABCD was constructed first. The diagonal DB was used to describe an arc that intersects the extended line DC at F. A vertical line from F produced a rectangle AEFD which has a harmonious relationship with ABCD. A further rectangle can be produced to points HI; this has a harmonious relationship with AEFD.

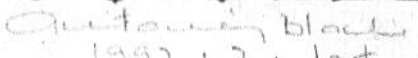

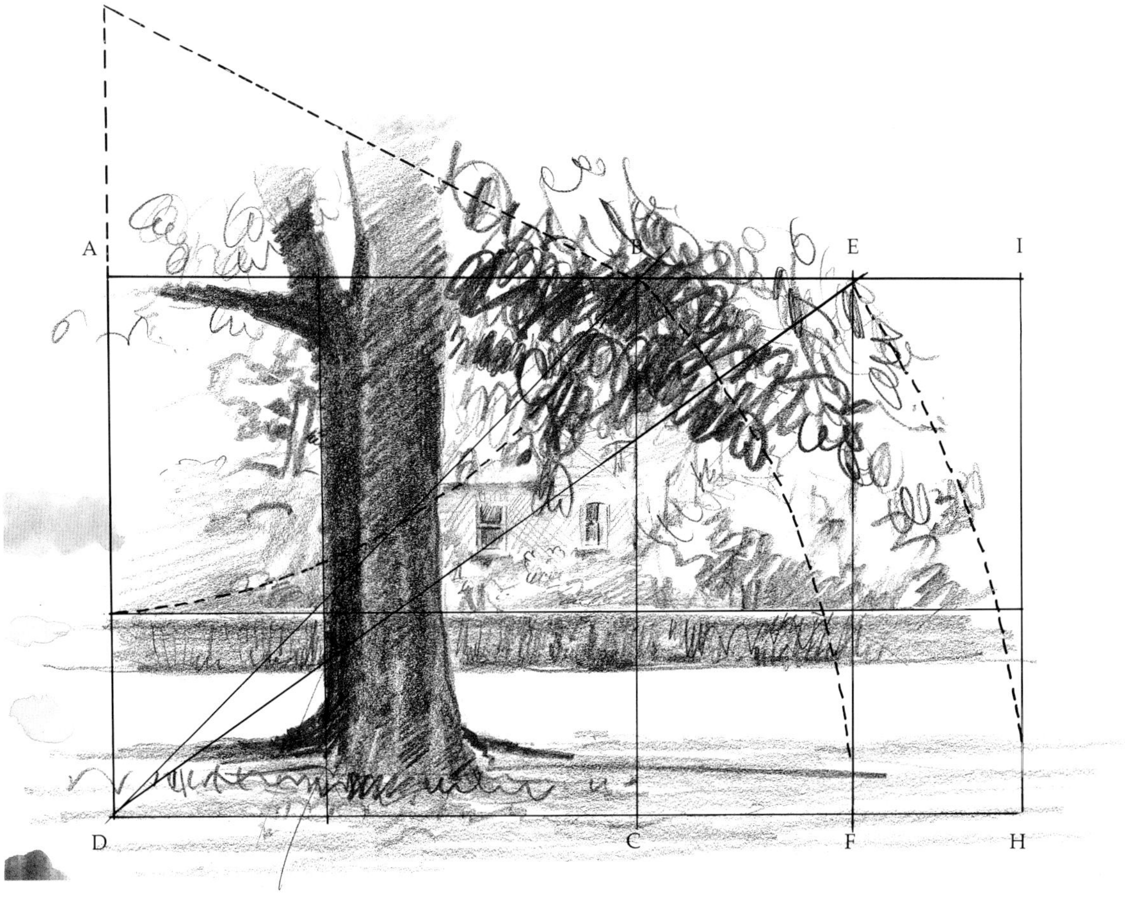

ABOVE
Antonia Black
White Jars
Gouache, 22×30 inches (56.3×76.8cm)
The large sheet of paper was first subdivided by tape into four sections. This enabled the artist to develop each idea from one painting into the next. The result is dynamic and decisively painted, showing a rhythm discovered by the blue line which details the arrangement and structure of the white jars. Each picture vigorously explores new arrangements and viewpoints of the subject. Color is added in uncomplicated washes so the focus of the idea, the blue line, can dominate.

terms, the rectangle that the subject forms on paper is divided in the proportion of approximately one third to two thirds, vertically and/or horizontally. The important elements of the composition are then placed on this intersection so that the final composition is balanced and harmonious.

Most people have a natural feeling for these proportions, perhaps because as an infant the first and most important shape in their lives was their mother's face, and in particular the eyes and mouth, both positioned in perfect harmony at one-third intervals on the face.

Another theory encouraged the artist to imagine that the rectangle of the canvas contained an oval, within which the important elements of the composition should be located, while the corners were left without any significance.

Squaring Up

This is a quick method of transforming a preliminary drawing into the main subject, at a different scale but with the same proportions (see below).

Working from Photographs

Photographs, used discriminatingly, are a very useful source of reference information, particularly for fast-moving subjects such as changes of light, animals or people. They can be used as prints in conjunction with on-the-spot drawings and notes. Photographs can be used to identify interesting viewpoints and composition ideas; a series of pictures taken around, above, close up and from a distance serve a similar purpose to thumbnail planning sketches. Details of texture, structure and color are also worth recording, and can be combined in the studio into the final painting.

Transparencies are another method of making a photograph which can then be projected on to the subject and parts of the image traced from them. This method should be treated cautiously as results can look flat and superficial. Copying information directly from a photograph or, worse still, a postcard is the weakest use of this medium.

The Tease-and-worry Book or Sketchbook

The sketchbook is a personal and invaluable tool for every artist. The word 'sketch' seems to suggest something which is superficial and trivial, whereas this book is used to collect information, observe, and analyze, develop ideas, make notes, doodle, and produce spontaneous imaginary experiments with color and new media. Sketchbooks are an essential working tool. They come in a range of sizes and paper qualities, with the advantage that they can be carried easily and used anywhere. Most artists will own a range of sizes and explore in them a variety of ideas, media and techniques.

RIGHT AND RIGHT BELOW
Antonia Black
Sangenjo, Gallicia, Spain
Watercolor
These carefully observed leisure craft and working boats summarize all the enjoyment of an idyllic seaside holiday. Each study is captured with a few selected lines and accents of color. They float in a sea of white space which is as vital to the mood as are the subjects.

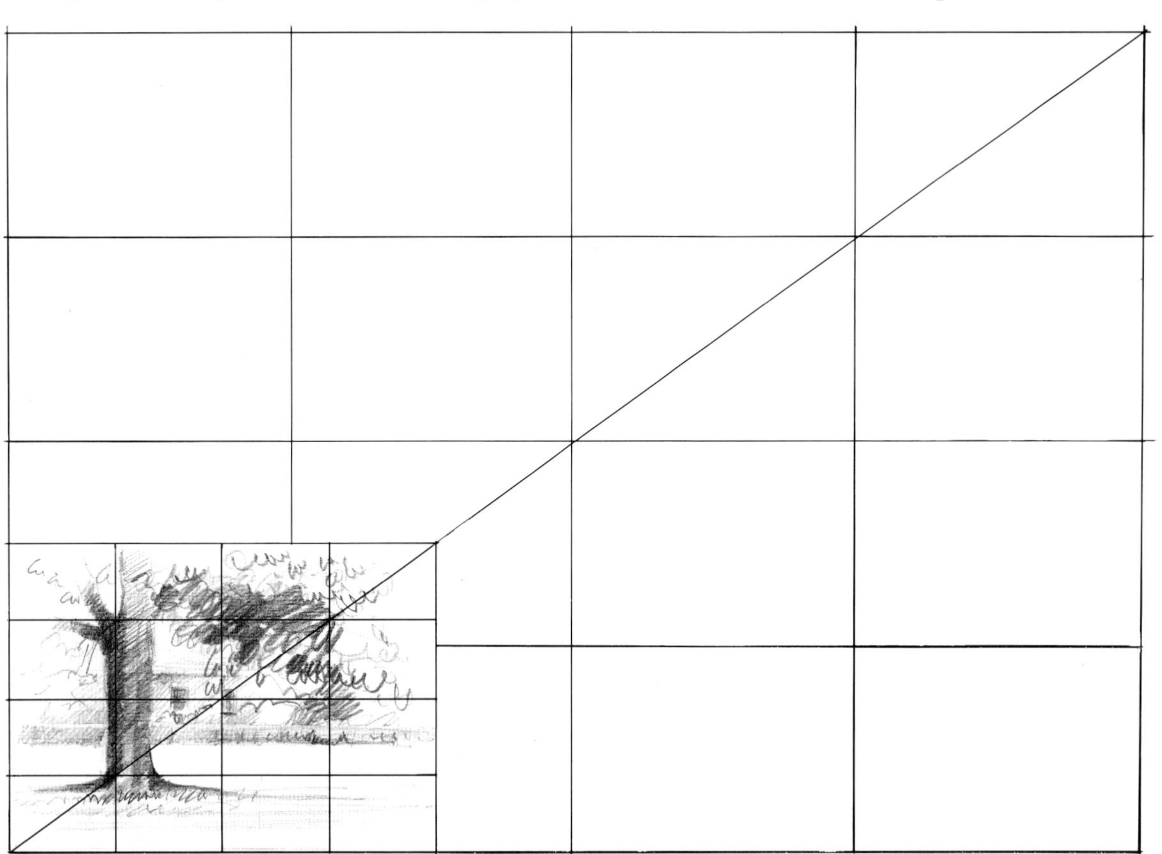

LEFT
Squaring up is a simple way of increasing the scale of a preliminary drawing to form the main work. Construct a grid as shown and use the diagonal to divide both surfaces. The image can then be transferred section by section from one to the other. If you are transferring information to watercolor paper, use only a light pencil guide or the marks may show through the paint. Avoid using an eraser as it will damage the surface of the paper.

The Working Drawing

Portability encourages the use of sketchbooks out on location, where copious working drawings and color notes can be made to be developed back in the studio. You will gradually develop your own methods of collecting relevant materials but this will not need to be a highly finished drawing. Several working drawings will be needed.

Ideas for composition, the structure and character of the subject, tone, color and texture can be drawn in small sections to be used as key references, These can be made fairly quickly on site then reassembled later. It can, for instance, take a long time to draw a tree in full detail, but if the larger shapes of the particular tree are noted, small detailed drawings can then be made of a few leaves or the bark, and notes about color added. Color can be difficult to describe but if it is related to familiar everyday objects, this can then be easily matched with pigment later. For example, the color of a bush might be the same as the bedroom curtains; a note is more use than any amount of verbal description. Good working drawings and references save hours of wasted time on site.

Sequencing Ideas

The landscape is constantly changing due to atmospheric conditions, and the play of light has always delighted artists. The Impressionists found endless techniques, colors and ideas to interpret the fleeting effects which can radically transform the subject.

Anita Young is an artist who loves to work in a similar way to the Impressionists. She enjoys working in the same place for long periods of time and finds endless inspiration in color, space, movement and form. She once spent a whole summer working from one field, and would have liked even more time, so rich was it in source material.

The sequence of paintings and drawing shown here were made in France at Fay sur Lignon. The pen and sepia ink drawings are spontaneous and direct, with abreviated marks denoting texture and pattern in the landscape. The paintings were not made from the drawings, but out on location. The results show selective and simple marks which activate the white paper and integrate it into the space and atmosphere of the paintings. The group of pictures show a feel for the light as it changes throughout the day, beginning with *Golden Hush*, when the details of the view are soft and indistinguishable due to rising mist. This is expressed with soft wet washes which seem to emerge from the paper, as the landscape

ABOVE
Anita Young
Golden Hush
Watercolor, 11½×16 inches (29.4×41cm)

BELOW
Anita Young
Play of Light
Watercolor, 10×14 inches (25.6×35.8cm)

seems to emerge into view. The second picture, called *Play of Light*, is bolder with the landscape clearly seen and enunciated, the painting crisp and the color strong. There is much detail and enjoyment of the language and pattern of the landscape. Brush marks are fertile and have a life of their own describing the form and structure of the view.

The painting entitled *Silent Song* shows the end of the day; the minimalist marks and washes of color summarize the disappearing landscape. The dark silhouettes of the trees try to hold on to the surface of the paper while the rest seems to be drawn back into it. The white space emerges as moonlight to lighten the dark, and is as vital as the simple brush marks; both are considered and controled. The result has a lyrical quality, conveying the mystery of an event that has happened daily since time began.

LEFT
The artist made a number of pen and sepia ink working drawings spontaneously on location. Through them, ideas for composition and details of the landscape could be analysed and translated on to paper with incisive marks using pen and ink (left). This medium encourages the artist to be confident and decisive for, once made, the marks cannot easily be altered. The paintings were also made on location rather than from the drawings alone.

BELOW
Anita Young
Silent Song
8×11½ inches
(20.5×29.4cm)

8. Further techniques

The chapter on Basic Techniques deals with the two fundamental skills essential to all types of watercolor media: how to work with board washes, and how to control the brush. The many subsequent examples of paintings in this book will demonstrate them to one degree or another. However there are many other ways of using the paint developed by artists who have experimented and 'played' with the media. These techniques are fun to experiment with either as individual exercises or to inspire an ongoing painting.

Starting a Painting

There are no fixed rules as to how to begin a painting; each artist will eventually find his own starting point and methods of developing his intentions. Beginning with broad simple areas and coming to the fine detail last is a standard method which is useful for the beginner. If the details of a painting are begun too quickly it is easy to loose sight of the picture as a whole, which can lead to distortions of space and a weak relationship between color and form.

The painting of a typical London park (far right) shows several stages that the artist should consider, and the order in which they should be painted.

1. The largest shapes are considered and painted first. In the landscape these are the sky and the land. They have been painted with wet graduated washes which work from yellow green to pale blue-green for the land, dark blue to pale pink for the sky. This immediately gives a sensation of the space between the artist or viewer and the furthest point, the horizon.
2. The next largest shapes are formed by the trees. A picture consists of background out of focus, midground some focus, and foreground full focus. The background trees are painted as one horizontal shape in blue-green. The midground and foreground trees are laid over this in a mid-tone wash. The

Favilla Baker
Barnes Common
Mixed media, gouache, acrylic and oil pastels, 22×30 inches (56.3×76.8cm)
This suburb of London has been given energy and life through the vigorous and spontaneous handling of the media, and the use of complementary pairs of reds and greens, and oranges and blues. The result is full of movement, the trees seeming to rustle in the breeze made by the bus as it moves through the picture.

The underpainting and composition are defined by large translucent fluid washes. These have been overwashed to develop the detail with either gouache or acrylics. The final lines and focal points, such as the red bus and the white railings, have been put in with oil pastel. This is suitable for use over any waterbased medium, but it should be used with great care. Oil and water are not good mixers, and the oil takes longer to dry than water-based paints, so the top layer of paint may crack up.

There is a strong use of black as a descriptive line. It serves as a color, and therefore helps the pigments to glow. It also contrasts well with the thicker lines of the white railings.

light areas are left unpainted.
3. The darks and dark halftones are painted over the top, giving a volume and structure to the trees. The paint is put on in marks which suggest the character of the trees.
4. The detail and foreground is then put in, with particular attention being given to the size and scale of the paintmarks. The closest ones, suggesting grass, are larger and more widely spaced than the ones further back.

Techniques with Wash

Once the basic techniques of laying a wash have been mastered, you can expand your skills in a variety of ways.

Under Painting

Surprisingly, this is a traditional method for watercolor, despite being associated with oil paint. The method is of particular value to the beginner because it allows the preliminary planning of the tones and structure of the composition to be clearly developed. Choose a pale color directly related to the subject as the color of the wash will affect the top colors slightly. The color and extent of the wash also acts as a linking base color, giving a sense of unity to the painting. Apply the underpainting with plenty of water and allow it to dry. In pure watercolor the white is left as unpainted paper.

Line and Wash

This technique has a wide range of applications from delicate botanical studies through to the energetic spontaneous figure work of such as Rembrandt and Rodin. The main trap to avoid is to make the image look drawn out then filled in, as this will look wooden and labored. Traditionally the line was drawn in first, then washes added later, but the technique is more energetic if the washes or colors are broadly laid in before adding line in either pen, fine brush, colored or wax crayons on top. The line should not outline the color, but rather the two should achieve independence of each other.

Glazes

This technique in pure watercolor is a method of laying one thin wash over another. It originated with the early oil painters, who built up beautiful rich color

ABOVE
Elaine Alderson
Trees
Watercolor, 15¼×12½ inches (39×32cm)
This painting of a London park show a common method of starting a painting, by painting in the largest shapes to give a framework and then increasing the detail. This is useful for the beginner; if details are begun too quickly it is easy to lose sight of the picture as a whole, which can lead to spatial distortion and a weak relationship between color and form.

LEFT
These examples of some of the more advanced techniques discussed on this and the following pages combine to form a work of art in its own right.

LEFT
Anita Young
The Path
Watercolor, 4¼×6¼ inches (10.9×16cm)
The scalpel can be used as constructively as the brush to reshape or alter a painting. In this example a painting has been sliced vertically and rearranged. This results in tantalizing glimpses of the subject, but with the focus of attention directed to the dynamics of the paintmarks, which impart a new order and space to the subject.

through painting one thin color over another. Glazing is also very suitable as a technique for acrylic because it dries very quickly. The resulting colors are far richer than an opaque mix because the white of the paper shines through, giving a luminosity to the color. There are media on the market which are sold for use with acrylics, either neat or diluted with water.

Textures

A whole range of rich and interesting textures can be achieved through a variety of techniques. The methods apply to all water-based paints unless otherwise stated.

Scumbling

This creates a texture through broken color effects. It is particularly suitable for gouache and acrylic. Very dry paint is scrubbed unevenly in all directions or in a circular motion over other layers of dry color, so that some of it shows through. The result should be rich and vibrant; light can be laid over dark or vice versa. A harder bristle brush is more suitable than a hair brush. Load the brush with paint and hold it against a rag or tissue to absorb excess moisture before using it.

Dry Brush

Load the brush with dry paint, blotting out any excess moisture. Hold the bristles between your thumb and forefinger to feather them out; a stiff bristle brush is best. The method is most effective if used selectively to suggest fine detail.

Stippling

Apply the paint with the point of the brush in a series of separate small marks. The Impressionist painters, and in particular Seurat, explored this technique using a wide range of dot sizes. The dots of paint can be laid over washes and the color and tone of each dot should be carefully considered before applying.

Brushmarks

Brushwork is generally associated with oil paint, but it has the same intrinsic value to watercolors in all media. If the size of brushmarks diminishes from foreground through to background, it can help to create the illusion of depth and space. Brushmarks leading into a painting can accentuate the perspective, while those following the contour lines can give form, solidity and modelling to an object. Foliage can be suggested with dry brush marks, and rain by working into a wet wash with a dry bristle brush to stroke the paint into swirls and squalls.

Splattering

This method is suitable for any type of watercolor or ink and is ideal for brightening up an even area of color, by using either a second contrasting color or one close in tone. Using an old toothbrush dipped into paint, hold it over the painting and pull a knife across the bristles so that the paint squirts off in a spray. Use newspaper to protect paints that do not need to be worked on. The spray is finer with thicker paint. The method is rather unpredictable so it is advisable to experiment first.

Blot

This technique is ideal for inks or very watery paint, which is dropped on to the painting from various heights from a brush or spoon. The board can be tipped to let runs develop, or the blot can be blown through a straw, or objects can be printed into the paint. The resulting marks can either be offset by blotting with another paper, or a mirror image can be formed by folding the paper on to itself.

Masking Techniques

These are methods of protecting the paper from paint. They can all be lifted off after use.

Masking Tape

This is ideal for straight lines and is stuck gently on to the paper. All waterbased paints and most techniques can be used against it, from flat thick paints to washes, splattering etc. The tapes are available in high and low tack forms. Paints must be dry before the tape is removed.

Paper

Cheap paper is cut either with a sharp craft knife or scissors into the required shapes then laid on the paper. Weights can be put on top to hold the paper steady if necessary.

Resists and Masking Fluids

These can be used with all waterbased media and are applied to the paper to protect the white areas. Masking fluid is a latex liquid and can be used with a brush or pen. It can be rubbed off after the paint is dry. Wax crayons or white kitchen candles can be used to draw directly on to the paper; when the surface is painted the watercolor slides off the waxed areas. The color of wax

BELOW
Kevin Chapman
The Late Light
Watercolor, 10×13¾ inches (25.6×35.2cm)
This simple yet evocative woodland scene is based on a combination of techniques, through which the luminosity and atmosphere of the woods emerge. Layers of washes in translucent and opaque watercolor are drawn into with inks, and sgraffito highlights. Depth in the painting is emphasized through the hot and cold color relationship of the warm foreground tone which changes into the cool blues of the background. The trees, their scale and relationship to each other, are classic examples of the elementary rules of perspective.

crayons remains vibrant and they can continue to be used throughout the painting. Further rich textures can be developed by scraping off the wax with a blade.

Wash-off

The design is made in either oil pastels or thick gouache then waterproof ink is flooded across them. After it has dried the paper is washed with warm water, so that the ink washes away in places, revealing the pastel or paint underneath.

Sgraffito

This technique involves removing dry paint so that the white paper is revealed; it should only be used on heavyweight papers of over 140lb (see page 12). Paint is scraped back with a craft knife to reveal white highlights. The effect is similar to dry brush and gouache. If the paper is very thick, whole sections of the top surface can be cut and carefully peeled out, revealing areas of white that can be left or re-marked. Thick paint such as acrylic or gouache can be scratched and cut in a similar way when dry.

Additives

These change the characteristics of the medium and can be used for specialized effects.

Gum Arabic

This can be added to all types of watercolor but is especially effective when added to inks. Together with gelatine or glycerine, it is used as a binder for the pigments. When painted on to the surface of a picture it will act as a form of varnish.

Soap

Mixing paint with soap has several functions. Firstly it has a similar effect to Gum Arabic, the paint becomes less fluid and shows up the brush marks. Soap can also help the paint to cover areas affected by grease on the paper. Finally real objects such as leaves and flowers can be covered with liquid soap before paint is applied over the top. The leaves can then be placed paint side down on the paper, covered with some greaseproof paper and then pressed carefully. The objects will leave an imprint.

Salt

Grains of salt dropped into wet paint will draw up the color, leaving white irregular marks on the paper. This can be left to dry, and then process repeated.

Blot off

The wet surface is blotted off with textured paper or cloth which leaves an imprint.

White Spirit or Oil

White spirit can be painted on to the surface and dried. When watercolor is laid over it it reacts, because oil and water will not mix, and the result is a marbled effect. White spirit will dry colorless and the smell will eventually evaporate.

Alcohol

When working outside during cold weather, a little alcohol will prevent the watercolors freezing. Paul Sandby, the father of English watercolor, is reputed to have added gin to his paints.

Alterations – Techniques

Making corrections is an intrinsic part of using any medium. Painting made from any of the waterbased medium, including pure watercolor, can be corrected and altered. Change is a vital component of the creative process, enabling the artist to realize and develop ideas throughout the period and process of making the painting. Techniques for changing the painting can be learned and practiced just as those for applying the paint. Most of the methods will apply to the whole range of media but a few are specific to one.

Lifting Paint

1. Blotting can be used for all media and is useful for when the paper becomes saturated with either water or paint. Excess moisture can be removed from large areas with sheets of blotting paper, small blots lifted with a dampened corner or a dampened twisted tissue; put the point directly into the centre of the blot to avoid it spreading.
2. Blots can also be lifted with cotton wool swabs or small sponges.
3. Large dry areas of paint can be lifted and almost totally erased with a dampened sponge. Moisten the area with clean water and, as the paint lifts, squeeze it out. The paper will retain a little stain from the pigment. A more drastic measure is to hold the whole paper under the tap, and sponging or blotting off excess moisture.
4. Smaller areas can be lifted off with a damp clean brush with all excess moisture squeezed from it.

RIGHT
Kevin Chapman
The Long Sea
Watercolor/gouache, 18×26 inches (46.1×66.6cm)
This moody and evocative painting uses a variety of techniques to create a powerful and realistic interpretation of the sea. Overlapping washes were laid in with large sponges and brushes. This results in a wonderful luminosity and a sensation of depth to the water. The space has been defined by using a Prussian blue mixed with vermilion to create a dark moody sky. This was washed on and then lifted off using dry tissue, and salt crystals were then dropped on to the damp paper to soak up even more pigment.
The white foamy crests of the waves have been dealt with by dabbing on thick gouache with a stiff brush and dry sponge, the thick paint teased into droplets with the end of the brush. After the paint dried, further flecks of white were made by using a sgraffito effect – scraping through the paint into the surface of the paper. Finally the most interesting area technically, the focus of the painting, is the breakwater. The top layers of the paper have been carefully cut out and peeled off, exposing the under layer, on to which the textural details of the wood have been painted. Thin sharp lines add to the texture created by the paint soaking into the cuts where the blade sliced into the paper.

RIGHT
Rosemary Williams
The Hedgerow
Inks and gouache,
This spontaneous painting was made on location. The forms and rhythms of a tangled hedgerow have been interpreted into abstracted marks and washes. The basic composition was laid in with diluted colored ink washes. These are waterproof, so when overlaid they make deep vibrant mixtures. The tendrils of the plants were drawn in with a pen and a stick, and the blossoms were dabbed on with very thick gouache and a tissue.

5. Hard edges left when a wash has dried can be softened with a moist brush used in a circular motion; the edge will eventually disappear and excess moisture blotted away.
6. Razor blades or craft knives can be used to scratch off small stubborn marks. Larger areas of paint can be scraped back, leaving the tooth of the paper, but adding more color may cause problems.
7. Whole sections of heavyweight paper can be sliced or torn out, leaving the underlayers of the paper to be re-worked.
8. A soft eraser is suitable for lightening delicate areas, but take care not to rub too hard.
9. Fresh white breadcrumbs are perfect for cleaning white areas of paper and removing faint pencil smudges.

Correcting Gouache

This is similar to watercolor. The only major difference is the opacity factor of the medium. Thick paint can be used to cover thinner and lighter areas. Darker areas are slightly more difficult and will need more than one coat of thick paint. Underpainting can be dampened, blotted and dried before thicker correction layers are used.

Correcting Inks or Liquid Watercolor

Correcting these is difficult as they sink well into the paper. To change large areas, a coat of acrylic or gouache may be used. Small blots and drips can be removed with a corner of damp blotting paper or scratched off with a blade.

9. Applications

The final section of this book contains a selection of works demonstrating the wide variety of popular themes and applications developed by watercolorists. Many of the professional artists whose works illustrate this book would probably say, when pressed, that they do not consciously follow these rules. Instead they will stress the importance of total enjoyment and involvement with the painting, their personal enquiry being the foremost priority. The rules and controls are used intuitively and may perhaps only be consciously applied when the results are criticized or evaluated, in order to develop or correct work in progress. Few artists will work out vanishing points or refer to color charts or lists of techniques at the start of a picture. The rules and controls have been learned, practiced and absorbed into the subconscious memory.

People

People in movement are a challenge for any artist, whatever their preferred media. It is best to begin by working from figures that are in stationary poses; traditionally the artist employed models to pose in the studio. But you must develop a more plastic or malleable way of working so that movements and changes of pose can be absorbed into the study. This is an important point, for it means that the priorities of the figure or pose are established first, then followed by more detailed modelling of volume and facial characteristics. Think of a figure looming out of the mist or walking towards you along a beach: the essential characteristics are determined by the general posture, overall size and shape of the figure, and the relationship of weight or center of gravity to the ground. Recognition is possible long before detailed features come into focus.

RIGHT
Francis Bowyer
Ladies of La Flotte
Watercolor 13½×9¾ inches (34.5×25cm)
This composition, based on simple diagonals and complementary color relationships of blue, orange, green and red, draws the eye to these stalwart ladies who are economically painted with few details, apart from acute attention to the quizzical tilt of the glasses, solid girth and the no-nonsense stance of arms and feet.

LEFT
Bernard North
Reclining Nude
Watercolor, 11½×16½ inches (29.4×42.2cm)
Reclining Nude is a delicate rhythmic study in pure watercolor that captures the pose without losing the feeling of life in the model. The basic forms and directional lines were lightly drawn. Color was added in two wet washes, pinky red for figure and background, then blue for the bed, with shadow areas being overpainted into pink wash. More intense colors were then fed into the wet washes to accentuate the volume and local color of the figure. Finally the dark overwash of the background helps to throw up the light areas of the figure, while the brushwork echoes the rhythm of the pose.

FAR LEFT
Kevin Chapman
Who, Me?
Watercolor, 13×19½ inches (33.3×49.9cm)
This is a rich and exotic mixed media study of a model posed in the studio. The color scheme is simple, based entirely on red and its complementary green; their interaction gives warmth and life to the subject and emphasis to the enigmatic and compelling green eyes.

LEFT
Antonia Black
Water Tennis
Watercolor, 12×9 inches (30.7×23cm)
This is a simple, very quick study painted with selected direct brush marks. The color is limited to ocher, cobalt and cerulean blue.

Still Life

This is a favorite subject for all artists, whatever their medium. The objects surrounding us are an endless source of inspiration, whether it be the rich opulence of fruit, game, flowers and vegetables as portrayed by the seventeenth-century Dutch School or the soup cans and packaging of Pop Art as immortalized by Andy Warhol. Still life as a subject became popular in its own right in the sixteenth century, following the demise of religious painting with the Reformation in northern Europe. Early examples still contain biblical references such as bread and water, or flowers and fruit that have hidden religious meanings, but still life soon became a standard way of showing off the skills of the artist in a secular context. The great period of Dutch still life was the seventeenth century, and many of its exponents specialized within the genre – Jan Breughel on flowers, for example. In the late nineteenth century Paul Cézanne chose still life for his innovatory structural experiments.

As a subject it is an ideal way for an artist to practice and develop basic skills of composition, colour and perspective and to explore techniques, as it is not vulnerable to fluctuations of taste or the vagaries of the weather and light. Subject matter can be gathered from any source and set up in a studio or painted in a location. Before starting, consideration should be given to the scale, color and texture of one object against another. The light source can bring atmosphere or sparkle to any set-up by controling the tones or throwing shadows across backgrounds or support.

Fruit and vegetables make a colorful subject, with interesting textures and shapes that are relatively simple to paint. They can be grouped to form interesting contours or studied individually. The composition and negative shapes should be considered carefully and the set-up looked at from several viewpoints. A strong composition is vital for any group, and objects must be placed carefully in relationship to the paper as well as each other.

BELOW
Antonia Black
Blue Bananas
Watercolor, 18×24 inches (46.1×61.4cm)
The bold flat pattern is painted with decisive marks of opaque gouache, each layer being allowed to dry before applying the next. The subject has been chosen, arranged and painted to exploit fully the pattern and rhythm of the objects. The result is bold, exciting and vigorous. The eye is swirled around and through the composition by the shapes and the colors. The perspective is deliberately distorted and the fruits boldly outlined in ultramarine blue so that any sense of atmosphere or realistic space is avoided, the emphasis being on the power of the pattern.

LEFT
Maggie Scott
Cherries For Tea
Watercolor, 19½×17½ inches (49.9×44.8cm)
This is a sensual painting which celebrates the partnership of composition and color. The rich luscious intensity of the violet/red cherries contrasts tonally with the large harmonious pastel washes in the background and foreground patterns. They are painted with swirls of intense pigment that capture tiny areas of white paper to create sparkling highlights. The stalks and leaves add character, while their random directions and complementary yellow/greens contrast energetically with the rest. Stability is created by the blue foreground triangle, leading the eye up and over the fruit to the blue horizon line that anchors the top of the painting.

LEFT
Antonia Black
Two Mangos
Watercolor, 19½×24 inches (49.9×61.4cm)
Antonia Black demonstrates that just two objects can make an interesting composition, through their relationship with each other and with the background. Just turning the fruit so that the colors are juxtaposed sets up a visual dialogue, which is further emphasized by the bold complementary color relationships of red, green and blue. The paint has been applied in broad washes, showing the underworking, and creates an atmospheric setting for the fruits. The brushwork and color intensity become tighter when describing the form and exotic colors and texture of the fruit.

LEFT
Stephanie Newland
Jay
Watercolor, 16×22 inches (41×56.3cm)
This jay was painted outside where it was found, its eyes still bright and feathers lustrous, freshly killed by a cat. These sensitive and compassionate studies are intuitively painted with free fluid washes and confident economical brushwork. The artist has scaled the size of the brushes to the proportions of the feathers and areas of fine detail. The studies investigate the beauty of the jay from three positions and come together in a rhythmic composition. The background stains and accidental splatters have been left; they add to the spontaneity of working outside. They could be removed if necessary by scraping or blotting them off.

Natural Forms

Images of flora and fauna began their development through the tomb and pottery decoration of the first civilizations, but observation from life was not made until the Chinese Han Dynasty around the birth of Christ. The advent of paper, first made in 105AD in China, was of momentous importance as a ground, complementing paintings on silk and damask. Illuminated manuscripts from medieval Europe are rich in ornamental animal and plant pictures. By the middle of the fifteenth century, however, realism began to surpass the imaginary and drawings by Pisanello (1395-1455) show remarkable observations of horses made from life. This new understanding flourished in the hands of Leonardo da Vinci and Albrecht Dürer, and also through the invention of printing and movable type. Today's artists follow on from these rich traditions, based on acute observation interpreted with technical skill, economy of line and sensitive and imaginative color mixture.

LEFT
Antonia Black
Amaryllis
Gouache, 21×14½ inches (53.8×37.1cm)
This is a simple incisive summary of this exotic plant. Total emphasis is on one bold confident and gestural mark, which simultaneously conveys the essence of the succulent stem and the spirit of watercolor. The flower has been left deliberately insignificant to enhance the power of and focus on this extraordinary stem.

LEFT BELOW
Josephine Newman
White Lily
Watercolor, 22×22 inches (56.3×56.3cm)
By comparison this painting is mysterious, yet organized and controled. The composition maximizes the value of the negative white space so that the leaves, stem and flowerheads can be seen to advantage. Details of color and structure are closely observed, then expressed with a selective palette in overlays of delicate tonal washes. Individual brushmarks are difficult to decipher, apart from the white highlights that give a succulence and life to the plant. The buds and half-open flower shyly turn from view, leaving much open to interpretation and allowing the focus of attention to turn to the leaves.

FAR LEFT
Hazel Penwarden
Nest with Autumn Leaves
Watercolor, 16×19¾ (50×50.6cm)
The power of this rich and atmospheric painting lies in its limited palette of colors, arranged in a circular composition of warm browns balanced against cool grays. The lines of the leaves and plants also direct the eye around the picture until it finds the treasure hidden in the nest. The bright sparkle of the cool blue eggs complements the warm orange/browns of the leaves. The colors are applied as overlays of luminous washes from the complementary duos of orange/blue and yellow/violet. The brushwork is considered and delicate yet freely applied, suggesting the rich texture of the wood, nest and leaves.

Abstraction

Developments in twentieth-century painting have paved the way for artists to explore virtually any approach to drawing or painting. Paintings which may seem at first glance to be abstract are often based on a figurative beginning and have gone through a metamorphosis within the boundary of the actual picture. Figurative associations can be found in the random and arbitrary shapes made, for example, by ink blots, water, clouds or fire. The distinction between what is abstract or figurative is a fine one. Abstract painting is made without recourse to illusion or definable subject matter; decisions about color or shape are made in relationship to each other, allowing the picture to have its own dynamic. The artist is free to concentrate solely on the interplay of any number of possibilities relating to color, geometry, mark making or self expression. Abstraction from the reality of nature implies transforming the original visual stimulus, through selection, simplification and manipulation, into new and harmonious arrangements of shape and color, while retaining a strong connection with the original subject.

BELOW
Maggie Scott
Evening Atlantic
Watercolor, 22¾×22 inches (58.2×56.3cm)
Here the enjoyment of the medium is coupled with a simple subject. The luminosity of the evening light is economically expressed with bold translucent washes. The focus of the composition, the boat, is left unpainted, its structure economically revealed with the minimum of color and brushwork as it lies serenely anchored between the harmonious waves of color.

The four paintings illustrated are all abstractions from a common starting point: water. Each artist has foregone preparatory drawing in favor of an intuitive spontaneous response to the subject. Exhaustive preliminary analysis can result in contrived wooden interpretations. Abstracting or selecting information from reality is an important stage in an artist's development, preventing slavish copying of the subject by putting the onus on decision-making within the painting itself. A painting exists long after its subject matter has disappeared or been dismantled. Color, shape and compositional relationships should therefore be developed independently of the subject. Abstraction also allows the artist to investigate individual obsessions, ideas or viewpoints stimulated by the subject. Maggie Scott and Antonia Black both respond to the rhythm and sensation of the sea, and value the power of white paper as an element in their compositions, while Rita Hodson and Anne Vassallo share an interest in reflection and refraction.

ABOVE LEFT
Anne Vassallo
Glass and Pear
Watercolor, 30×22 inches (76.8×56.3cm)
This is a very large painting of a small section of still life. The paint is applied with a decorator's brush in bold economical gestures which add to the dynamics of the simple composition. The subject matter is not immediately obvious because of the economy of shape, color and gesture.

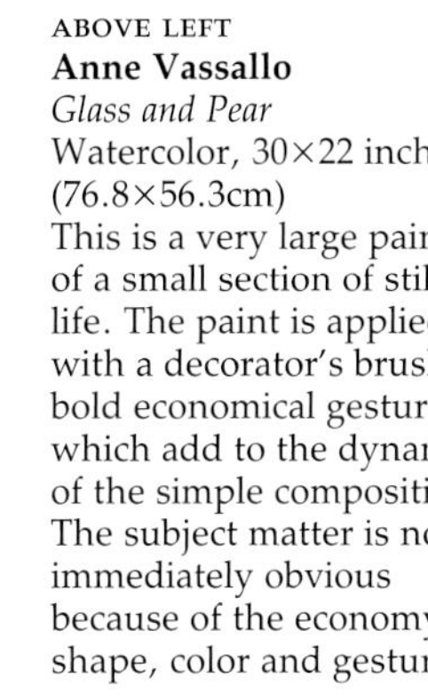

ABOVE RIGHT
Antonia Black
Houlgate
Watercolor, 6¾×9½ inches (17.2×24.3cm)
This subject is abstracted through the fluid and minimal simplicity of the composition. The economical brushmarks are isolated individually against the white paper, creating an impression of seascape and houses. The rough surface of the paper is enhanced by the granulated washes of cerulean and ultramarine blue so that its texture suggests the sparkle and movement of the sea.

LEFT
Rita Hodson
Spanish Chairs
Watercolor, 13×18½ inches (33.2×47.3cm)
At first glance this painting seems upside down, and as a composition it could work either way. The complex reflections of wrought iron chairs in a swimming pool are held together by the strong arch of blue created by the edge of the pool.

New Design Directions

Water-based paints and inks are much used by designers, as well as fine artists; both versatile and quick-drying, they offer a range of qualities that the designer can integrate into the planning process. The constraints, techniques and rules that apply to fine artists also apply to glazes, dyes, enamels, glass, fabric, metal and clay. The watercolor medium becomes a synthesis of the separate parts, for example, color, structure or texture. These can both inspire and influence the development of the design from the drawing board through to the finished work in more complex media.

Claire Ireland and Corinne Burton both make many careful preliminary studies in waterbased paints prior to translating their ideas into glazes, but both artists avoid directly copying the initial studies into the glazes. Ideas and designs repeated accurately will look stale and lack the spontaneity and vigor of the first interpretation. Elaine Alderson in her costume ideas has very different priorities; these direct, bold and lively studies reflect and encapsulate the mood and character of the play. The costumes are rarely seen in close up and theatrical budgets are always limited, and so the designer must work with flair and economy from the onset of ideas in the initial designs through to its final production. Rich detailing can be improvised using cheap textural items which are painted or sprayed to look real to the audience.

ABOVE
Elaine Alderson
Costume Designs for 'Lulu'
Watercolor, 20¾×27 inches (57×69.1cm)

LEFT
Corinne Burton
Iris Doronicum
Painted porcelain, 11½×11½ inches (29.4×29.4cm)
Painting on porcelain is a technically challenging process which the artist must master together with the skills and demands of drawing and design. The composition of *Iris Doronicum* is created with asymmetrical arcs of color that echo the curve of the plate. Each flower has been carefully analyzed and the observations translated into layers of glazes. The lush textural qualities and structure of the petals and leaves are drawn with empathy and fine detail.

LEFT AND RIGHT
Claire Ireland
Fishy Wall Piece with Leafy Shapes and Curly Copper, Clay and Wire
16×16×1 inches (41×41×2.6cm)
The gouache and ink design for the *Fishy Wall Piece* works as both a preparatory design for the clay relief, and as a decorative painting in its own right. Each area of the design is controled, and the pattern of colors and texture accurately positioned, so that when transferred to the clay the artist can lay in each area with decisive and fluid marks.

ABOVE LEFT
Corinne Burton
Pansy
Watercolor, 8×6 inches (20.5×15.4cm)
This charming watercolor study of a pansy is a fine observation of the flower, painted with heightened color and the emphasis on its structure and pattern. The painting is a good example of a preparatory analytical study in overlaid color washes with controled brushwork, which is then translated into glazes for the porcelain painting.

ABOVE
Glynis Porter
Fandango, The Dance of Love
Watercolor, 9×10×1 inches (23×25.6×2.6cm)
Three-dimensional watercolors are unusual, as are ones with a whimsical humor. This enchanting interpretation of the fandango has both. Pure watercolor techniques of wet into wet and translucent washes give a rich setting to this energetic dance. The figures are cut out of stiff watercolor paper and supported away from the background on wooden struts, so that they remain suspended in the animated expression of their love.

Index

Figures in *italics* refer to illustrations

Acknowledgments

The publisher would like to thank David Eldred, who designed this book; Pat Coward, who indexed it; and Jessica Hodge, the editor. We would also like to thank the following individuals, agencies and institutions, who loaned original artwork and/or supplied photographic material.

Addison Gallery of American Art, Phillips Academy, Andover, MA: page 11 (1943.30, gift of the artist)
Elaine Alderson: pages 19, 25, 78
Art Institute of Chicago: page 31 top (Alfred Stieglitz Collection, 1949.895)
Favilla Baker: page 64
Antonia Black: pages 17, 21, 48, 59, 61, 70, 72, 73, 75, 77
Sally Blenkinsop: page 36
Francis Bowyer: pages 55, 71
Corinne Burton: pages 78, 79
Kevin Chapman: pages 16, 27, 38, 44, 57, 67, 69, 70
Christies, London/Bridgeman Art Library: page 9 below
Devonshire Collection, Chatsworth House, Derbyshire. Reproduced by permission of the Trustees of the Chatsworth Settlement: page 30
Brian Fielding: page 56
Herbert Folwell: page 36
Haags Gemeentemuseum: page 45 below
Rita Hodson: pages 35, 57, 77
Claire Ireland: pages 78, 79
Liz Knutt: page 19
Metropolitan Museum, New York, Bergreuen Klee collection: page 62
Joan Milroy: page 46
Musée Nationale d'Art Moderne, Centre Pompidou, Paris: page 10
Stephanie Newland: page 74
Josephine Newman: page 75
Bernard North: page 70
Hazel Penwarden: page 75
Glynis Porter: page 79
Maggie Scott: pages 50, 73, 76
Tate Gallery, London: page 10 below
Jill Tweed: page 37
Anne Vassallo: pages 42, 77
By courtesy of the Board of the Trustees of the Victoria and Albert Museum: page 39 top;/Bridgeman Art Library: 8, 9, 49
Rosemary Williams: 16, 33, 35, 47, 69
David Wise: pages 7, 22, 28, 29, 52, 53
Yale University Art Gallery, New Haven: page 34 (1960.9.1)
Anita Young: pages 20, 62, 63, 66